The New York Times

CROSSWORDS TO BOOST YOUR BRAINPOWER
75 Crosswords to Sharpen Your Mind, Improve Your Crossword Skills, and Increase Your Vocabulary

Edited and with an Introduction by Will Shortz

ST. MARTIN'S GRIFFIN ✖ NEW YORK

Concept by SVH

ISBN 0-312-32033-7

First Edition: October 2003

10 9 8 7 6 5 4 3 2 1

INTRODUCTION

Among all the varieties of puzzles in the world, the crossword is the only one that regularly appears without instructions on how to do it. The solver is simply presumed to know.

The concept of the crossword is certainly simple: Enter answers to the definitions in the correspondingly numbered spaces in the grid, one letter per square, to complete an interlocking pattern of words across and down.

And yet . . . modern American crosswords have many specialized rules, conventions, and twists that are not obvious to the beginning or intermediate solver.

I'm reminded of a magazine editor in Honolulu a few years ago who decided to try his publication's crossword for the first time, and he wrote about encountering his first clue ending with a question mark. What did it mean, he wondered—that the clue might be true, but then again, it might not? That the information in it was actually wrong? He had no idea.

Recently on the *New York Times*'s on-line crossword forum, a solver commented on the clue "Of interest to collectors, say." The answer was RARE. The solver thought that FARE would have been better. Someone else pointed out that FARE in this sense is a noun and the clue called for an adjectival answer, so FARE could not have been correct, never mind whether it was "better" or not.

I thought how much harder the FARE solver was making the challenge for himself by not knowing that clues and answers must be in the same part of speech!

At last, here is a book that explains, for the first time in one place, all the ins and outs of solving modern American crosswords. It contains seventy-five puzzles from the daily *New York Times,* arranged in approximate order of difficulty, from Mondays (moderately easy) at the beginning to Saturdays (very difficult) at the end. Two clues in each puzzle, which are marked by *, come with annotations. Turn to the Hints and Tips section before the answers in the back of the book to get assistance in solving them. The hints are of a general enough nature that they will help you solve similar clues in other puzzles—both in this book and elsewhere.

As you proceed through the puzzles, I guarantee that you'll become a faster, smarter, more understanding solver. I think you'll derive more pleasure from doing crosswords, too, which is the ultimate goal.

Thanks to Frank Longo, one of the country's top puzzlemakers, for his help in preparing this book.

—Will Shortz

ACROSS

1 "Yikes!"
6 Actor Mineo and others
10 Aug.'s follower
14 Sound thinking
15 Strung tightly
16 The O'Hara homestead
17 Catastrophic event
19 "How sweet ___!"
20 Camera shot that gets all the details
21 Logos
23 Knob site
25 Sicilian erupter
* 26 Phi ___ Kappa
30 Chauffeurs
33 "I was out of town at the time of the murder," e.g.
35 Tree with cones
36 Neon or oxygen
39 Locale for a 17-Across
43 Underhanded
* 44 Raise ___ (cause a ruckus)
45 Soup seasoning
46 The South and the Southwest
49 Right away, on a memo
50 Messy dresser
52 Partner of 4-Down
54 Song starting "My country, 'tis of thee"
57 Team heads
62 An arm or a leg
63 It might follow a 17-Across
65 ___ vera
66 ___ Rabbit
67 Vietnam's capital
68 Mailed

69 Princes, e.g.
70 In regard to

DOWN

1 Con Ed power: Abbr.
2 Hockey score
3 Soil: Prefix
4 Morse marks
5 Flight board, e.g.: Abbr.
6 Daze
7 Car owners' org.
8 An apostle
9 Plant part
10 Clowns' props
11 Consumed
12 Kind of ballerina
13 Soviet news service
18 Part of Q.E.D.
22 Deprived (of)

24 Matured, as fruit
26 Lowest voice
27 Airline to Israel
28 Minuscule
29 Lawyers' org.
31 By way of
32 Lt.'s inferior, in the Navy
34 Evil spirits
36 Fellows
37 ___ mater
38 Stair part
40 Newsman Rather
41 Tease
42 "I have an idea!"
46 Cold dessert
47 Ones stringing up shoes
48 Thunder god
50 Photographer's request
51 Scent in furniture polish

53 Alexander, for short
54 "What a shame"
55 Taxis
56 1960's activist's hairdo
58 Detective Charlie
59 Sharpen
60 Supply-and-demand subj.
61 Comical playlet
64 Perfect rating

by Andrea C. Michaels

2   NO BIGGIE

ACROSS

1 Tobacco mouthful
5 Potato
9 Commercial makers
14 Swearing-in words
15 —- Vista (Web search engine)
16 Part of a gay refrain
17 Mozart's "Medamina," e.g.
18 New arrival on a horse farm
19 Nonsensical
20 Fibs of song
* 23 Movie locations
24 Shakespearean prince
25 High-spirited
28 The "p" in m.p.g.
30 Part of a cowboy's boot
34 Someone — (not mine or yours)
35 Give permission
37 Sacagawea coin denomination
38 Boy in a nightgown, in a children's rhyme
41 A Gabor sister
* 42 Closes in on
43 Cuts down, foodwise
44 Not so much
46 Campers, for short
47 Main course
48 As well
50 Snare
51 Waterspout habitue
59 Capt. Ahab's obsession
60 Tabula —
61 Bat's home

62 Where Van Gogh cut off his ear
63 Gershwin's "__ Plenty o' Nuttin' "
64 Baby-bouncing place
65 Elvis's Blue shoe material
66 Mercedes-—
67 Lost buoyancy

DOWN

1 Anthracite, e.g.
2 Mata — (spy)
3 Going strong
4 "How's tricks?"
5 Football 2-pointer
6 Prepares ground for planting
7 Rocky Mountain state

8 Limp-watch painter
9 Bamboozled
10 Dentists' tools
11 French Sudan, today
12 Vogue rival
13 Votes against
21 Allows entry
22 Dice roll
25 Gem
26 Advil competitor
27 "— directed"
28 Twosomes
29 View finders?
31 Bluffer's game
32 Bring together
33 Dodger shortstop of old
35 Many a Balkan
36 Abduct
39 "Vive __!"

40 Overdoes the criticism
45 Did salon work
47 Imitation
49 Like a 500-pounder
50 1980's–90's ring champ
51 "__ only trying to help"
52 Drive-—
53 After-Christmas event
54 Chicago paper, briefly
55 Wise one
56 Author Richard Henry __
57 Not odd
58 Smell horrible

SPUR #H_L

by Manny Nosowsky

ACROSS

1 Fellow
5 Contented
9 Noise at a street protest
14 Film part
15 Put on the payroll
16 Mandel of "St. Elsewhere"
17 Aid in crime
18 Look at flirtatiously
19 Make reparations
20 Alternative to briefs
23 Barbie's guy
24 Baseball great Mel
25 Says
27 Russian villas *dachas*
31 Change, as a hemline
33 Brand of sweetener
34 Leave out *OMIT*
35 Singer Paul
39 First newspapers on the street
42 Like most basketball stars
43 Decorative vases
44 Victorious
45 Chose *OPTED*
47 Beginnings
48 Drunk as a skunk
51 Animal that beats its chest
52 Superman foe ___ Luthor
53 Part of a girl's sock hop attire
60 Believe without question
62 Young Lennon
63 Pulitzer-winner James
64 "Purple" writing
65 Disabled
66 Place for an earring *LOBE*

67 President before Polk
68 Skunk's defense *SPRAY*
69 Cenozoic and Paleozoic, e.g.

DOWN

1 Taurus : Bull :: Cancer : ___
2 Penniless person
3 Trebek of "Jeopardy!"
4 Townshend of the Who
5 Haunted house inhabitants
6 Traffic controller
7 Singer Guthrie
8 Stag or hart
9 Celibate
10 Sexy *HOT*
11 Came to

12 Frisco footballer
13 New drivers, usually
21 Willy Wonka creator Dahl
22 ___-frutti
26 Choo-choos
27 ___ of gratitude
28 Greenish-blue
29 Select
30 Venerate
31 Change, as the Constitution *AMEND*
32 Jar-tops
34 Folklore meany
36 Post-It, e.g. *NOTE*
37 Windsor or sheepshank
38 Venomous snakes
40 Perform better than
41 Answering machine signals

46 Waiter's offering
47 First game of a doubleheader
48 Caught some Z's
49 Very sad
50 Praise
51 San Antonio landmark
54 Norway's capital
55 Not working, as a battery
56 Cabbagelike vegetable
57 Dr. Frankenstein's helper
58 Singer McEntire
59 Golf shop purchase
61 Employ

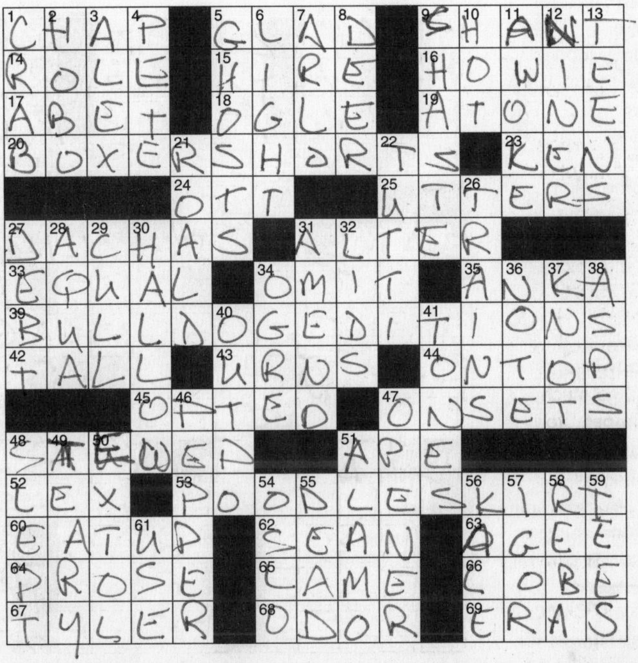

CHASTE
S_ _ STE

by Peter Gordon

SIEWED A_OKE

Grid solution (handwritten):

C	H	A	P		G	L	A	D		S	H	A	N	I
R	O	L	E		H	I	R	E		H	O	W	I	E
A	B	E	T		O	G	L	E		A	T	O	N	E
B	O	X	E	R	S	H	O	R	T	S		K	E	N
			O	T	T			L	T	E	R	S		
N	A	C	H	A	S		A	L	T	E	R			
E	Q	U	A	L		O	M	I	T		A	N	K	A
B	U	L	L	D	O	G	E	D	I	T	I	O	N	S
T	A	L	L		U	R	N	S		O	N	T	O	P
		O	P	T	E	D		O	N	S	E	T	S	
S	A	U	S	E	D		A	P	E					
L	E	X		P	O	O	D	L	E	S	K	I	R	T
E	A	T	U	P		S	E	A	N		A	G	E	E
P	R	O	S	E		L	A	M	E		L	O	B	E
T	Y	L	E	R		O	D	O	R		E	R	A	S

4 CONFIDENTIALLY SPEAKING

Myrrh

ACROSS

1 It may be high or low on a car
5 Immediately, to a surgeon
9 Little bits
14 Airport outside Paris
15 Brain tests: Abbr.
16 Book that's read word-for-word
17 Docking spot *Port*
18 Waterproof cover
19 Black, on a piano
20 Entry requirement, sometimes
*23 Headlight?
24 Little 'un
25 Uncle __
28 Retaliate
31 Hot springs
34 Bowie's weapon
36 "Mo' Better Blues" director Spike
37 Money man Greenspan
38 Spy
42 Fibster
43 Color
44 Watermelon throwaways
45 "__ Misérables"
46 Popular place
49 Take care of a bill
50 Diving seabird *Auk*
51 Fair-sized field
53 Buried loot
60 Stored on board
61 Like some testimony
62 Surgery souvenir
63 Lagoon encloser
64 Decorate anew
65 __ mater
66 Brawl *melee*
67 Shake hands for the first time *Meet*
68 Chatters

DOWN

1 Conks
2 Buffalo's lake
3 Actor Guinness
4 Gift of the Magi
5 Agree out of court
6 Kitchen whistler
7 Taj Mahal's city
8 Dosage amts.
9 Utilized
10 Brainless one
11 Composer Stravinsky
12 Curve
13 Hog's home
21 Raring to go
22 Wield a wheel
25 Brain protector
26 Comics orphan
27 King with a golden touch
29 Santa's assistants
30 Churchill's sign
31 What a new parent craves
32 Bamboo eater
33 On pins and needles
35 __-de-lance
37 Space __ (modern)
39 Auto airflow regulator
40 Over's partner
*41 Ad __ (to the stars): Lat. *AD AS*
46 Football strategy session
47 Memorial Day event
48 American wildcat
50 Fred's dancing sister
52 English paper
53 Love's opposite
54 Matinee hero
55 Test standard
56 Squirrel's home
57 Bruins' sch.
58 Freeway access
59 Historic times
60 On the __ (fleeing)

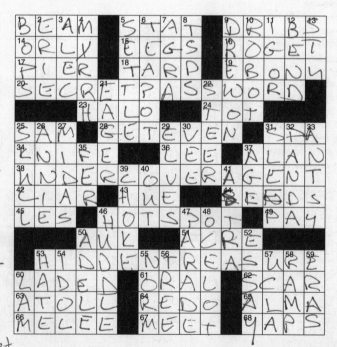

Grid fill:
Row 1: B E A M — S T A T — D R I B S
Row 2: O R L Y — E E G S — R O G E T
Row 3: P I E R — T A R P — E B O N Y
Row 4: S E C R E T P A S S W O R D
Row 5: — — — H A L O — T O T — — —
Row 6: S A M — G E T E V E N — S P A
Row 7: K N I F E — L E E — A L A N
Row 8: U N D E R C O V E R A G E N T
Row 9: L I A R — H U E — S E E D S
Row 10: L E S — H O T S P O T — P A Y
Row 11: — — A U K — A C R E — — —
Row 12: H I D D E N T R E A S U R E
Row 13: L A D E D — O R A L — S C A R
Row 14: A T O L L — R E D O — A L M A
Row 15: M E L E E — M E E T — Y A P S

by Marjorie Berg

ACROSS

1 Gather
6 Talk glowingly about one's children, e.g.
10 Doctrines, informally
14 Devastation
15 Prom-night transportation
16 Twirl
17 Say four-letter words
18 Makes choices
19 Mrs. Chaplin
20 The rain goes ___
23 Feather
25 Spray can
26 The horse goes ___
29 Blockhead
30 Kind of wrestling
31 Socially challenged
35 Desserts with crusts
37 Cheapskate
40 Red Cross supplies
41 Throat ailment
43 Film director Kazan
45 Ely of Tarzan fame
46 The church bells go ___
50 It's between Mars and Saturn
53 Military barker
54 20-, 26- or 46-Across, e.g.
57 "Blue" or "White" river
58 Frost
59 Mr. Spock portrayer
63 English school since 1440
64 Satan's work

65 Mortimer who was asked "How can you be so stupid?"
66 Method: Abbr.
* 67 Depend (on)
68 Russian despots

DOWN

1 Cries at fireworks
2 Gaping mouth
3 Caesar's hello
4 Get all sudsy
5 Is frugal
6 Rorschach presentation
7 Like a yellow banana
8 Military vehicle for landing assault troops
9 Absolute truth
10 Some are radioactive
11 Leopard features
12 Sal of "Exodus"
13 Guard dog's greeting
21 Prepare to hit a golf ball
22 Elvis's middle name
23 Braid
24 Inmate who's never getting out
26 The finest
27 1979 nuclear accident site: Abbr.
28 Like oxen pulling a plow
32 Hook up again
33 Pilotless plane
34 Yin's partner
36 Lees

38 "Xanadu" rock group, for short
39 Get the suds off
42 Sandwich bread
44 Anti
47 Lower
48 Phonograph needle's place
49 Sink outlets
50 Tommy Lee or James Earl
51 Agreement
52 Pullover shirts
55 Mop's companion
56 Alternative to Charles de Gaulle
* 60 "Culpa" starter
61 Hockey's Bobby
62 QB's gains: Abbr.

by Gene Newman

ACROSS

1 "___ for the poor"
5 German author Hermann
10 Iridescent gem
14 Lamb : sheep :: kid :
15 Crowning points
16 Whitish
17 Horrible boss
18 Unexpected benefits
19 They may be smoked or pickled
20 1974 Mel Brooks comedy
23 Fancy drinking glass
24 Optometrist's interest
25 Common name for sodium hydroxide
26 As well
27 Wettish
30 New moon, e.g.
32 Gumbo ingredient
34 Halloween cry
35 ___ constrictor
36 1959 film with Marilyn Monroe
41 Suffix with Paul
42 To do this is human
43 In for the night
45 Whitish
48 Fix up
50 Susan of "The Partridge Family"
51 Norma ___ (Sally Field role)
52 Raises, as the ante
55 Military greeting
57 Best Picture of 1981
61 It's hard to believe
* 62 Baby grand, e.g.
63 Guardianship
65 More than annoys
66 Distant planet
67 Particular
68 Apple carrier
69 Divvy up
70 Turner and Danson

DOWN

1 In the past
2 Ships' records
3 ___ Man (classic ad figure)
4 Great buy
5 Fit for living
6 Supply-and-demand subj.
7 Grimy air
8 Have a hunch
9 Think piece
10 ___ page (place for a 9-Down)
11 Spanish dish with rice
12 Bowling spots
13 Apartment dweller
* 21 A's opposite, in England
22 Bus station
23 1960's Pontiac muscle car
28 "You don't mean me?!"
29 Game played with a straight . . . or a straight face
31 Big laugh
33 French friend
35 Place for a claw
37 World-weariness
38 Before, to a bard
39 Bull-headed
40 Was on the brink
44 Blonde's secret, maybe
45 Extremely cold
46 Libyan expanse
47 Doctor
49 Stumblebum
53 The old man
54 Silence
56 Permissible
58 Take it easy
59 "Herzog" author Bellow
60 Latch ___ (get)
64 Ens' preceders

by Mitch Komro

CONSTANT REMINDERS   7

ACROSS

1 Dept. of Labor division
5 Be ill-humored
9 Bloodhound's clue
14 Erupt
15 Shortly
16 Handles the situation
17 Go around the internet
18 Monopoly equipment
19 Ralph's wife, on "The Honeymooners"
20 Nonstop
23 1970 Kinks hit
24 Rooster's mate
25 Little League coach, often
28 Firefighter, at times
31 Sault ___ Marie
34 Change with the times
36 Broke bread
37 Fisherman's bucketful
38 Nonstop
42 Willy of "Free Willy"
43 Perceive
44 Suitably
45 Hillary Clinton, ___ Rodham
46 ___ tank
49 Sushi fish
50 Instigate litigation
51 Spring bloom
53 Nonstop
60 Main impact
61 Ill-mannered
62 Lasso
63 "Last ___ in Paris"
64 Comparable
65 Submachine guns
66 Out-and-out
67 Sugar source

68 Repressed, with "up"

DOWN

1 Mount in Greek myth
2 It's used with a "giddyup!"
3 Medal recipient
4 More than bad
5 Word before shoe or soap
6 #19 of the Colts
7 ___ Ness
8 Where a cap is found on the body
9 Tackle box gizmo
10 ___: SINKER
11 Grand in scale
12 Bottle part
13 When doubled, an African fly

21 Toward cooler weather, say
22 "Give me an A . . .," e.g.
25 Matt of "The Talented Mr. Ripley"
26 Like a lot
27 "Shall we ___?"
29 Handle the food for a party
30 Rocky Mountain Indian
31 "À votre ___" (toast)
32 Card catalogue entry
33 Kind of alcohol
35 Kind of meeting at a school
37 Certain jazz
39 Pale-faced

40 Service charge
41 Pokémon card collecting, e.g.
46 Gentleman caller
47 Annapolis student
48 Gung-ho
50 "The Playboy of the Western World" author
52 Pancake topper
53 "Doggone it!"
54 Em, to Dorothy
56 Deadly missile
57 Trickle
58 ___ arms (angry)
59 Audition
60 A.C. capacity

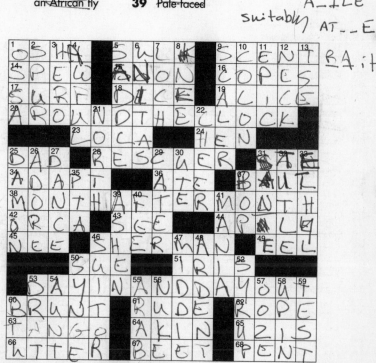

by Gregory E. Paul

8 ONE ON THE KISSER

ACROSS

1 What an umbrella may provide *(Shade cover)*
6 Moolah *(cash)*
10 Mama's partner
14 Dead, as an engine
15 Gallic girlfriend
16 Appliance with a cord and a board
17 Hole-____
18 Head-butts
19 Former Speaker Gingrich
20 Office fasteners
22 "Trick" joint
23 Symbol of slowness
24 Some Romanovs
25 Stir-fry pan
28 Former Detroit auto inits.
29 Belgian composer Jacques
31 Safe to eat
33 Not rigid
37 Gaucho's weapon
38 Neighbor of Egypt
40 Docking spot
41 Vegetable with a head *(cost)*
43 Went ape
45 "Kiss Me, ___"
46 Norm: Abbr.
47 Opposite of NNW
48 Embezzlement, e.g.
51 Battery terminal
* 53 Rock's partner
54 They're seen in air traffic control towers
59 Nay sayer
60 Dinner from a bucket

61 Foil maker *(Alcon)*
62 Chicken site
63 "Psycho" actress Miles *(Vera)*
64 Members of a pride *(Lions)*
65 Sea eagles
66 Locked (up) *(pent)*
67 Raises some interest?

DOWN

1 Pass over
2 Czech tennis ace Mandlikova
3 Each
4 Sand drifts
5 Unending
6 Scampi seasoning *(cheese)*
7 Memo from a dot-com, maybe
8 Not having much body *(flat)*
9 Actress Harper
10 Fires
11 "Gladiator" setting
12 Major nation
13 Pays to play
21 King Arthur's home
24 Gore-____ (fabric)
25 "Dragnet" star
26 What the nose knows *(kilo)*
27 Prefix with hertz
29 Round-the-world traveler Nellie
30 One with a lot to offer?
32 Reverse springs
33 J. Edgar Hoover's org.

34 Computer units
35 Hawaiian neckwear
36 One-named Art Deco designer ____ de France
39 Jazz man
42 Jazz man
44 Eccentric
46 Speak sharply to
48 Not do original drawings
49 "Employee of the Month," e.g.
* 50 Pop-rocker John
51 Deck out
52 "Dallas" matriarch Miss ____
54 Invitation request
55 Toward shelter
56 Computer image
57 Frog's home
58 Back talk *(sass)*

by Marjorie Berg

Libya -D-R-
Lyb
ODDBALL

ACROSS

1 Slightly open
5 African-American
10 Pay, as the bill
14 1953 Leslie Caron musical role
15 Spine-tingling
16 "Picnic" playwright
17 "And that's that!"
19 Partner of void
20 Outer: Prefix
21 See 4-Down
22 Evade, with "out of"
24 Kind of bag
25 ___ weevil
26 ___ corpus
29 Routine
33 Unreactive
34 Madam
35 Peak in ancient Palestine
36 "Go, ___!"
37 Doesn't just diet
38 School zone sign
39 Former Atlanta arena
40 Second voice
41 Spin
42 When both hands are together
44 Treasure locales
45 Open to the breeze
46 Wedding cake feature
47 Carry all over the place
50 Throws a shot
51 Bandleader Brown
54 Come into view
55 Not plan A or B, or even X or Y
58 ___ mater
59 "Farewell, François"
60 Exhort

61 Adult-to-be
62 Approvals
63 Egg-holder

DOWN

1 Sheltered, at sea
2 Give bad luck
3 Beefy actor Ray
4 With 21-Across, a 1970 John Wayne film
5 Makes soused
6 Do not disturb
7 Suffix with buck
8 Geom. figure
9 Index entries
10 It's given to Regis Philbin
11 Responsibility
12 Look at lustfully
13 Be a snitch
18 Parade sight
23 Lodge member
24 Michael Crichton novel, with "The"
25 Greet ceremoniously
* 26 Make a pass at
27 Prefix with -meter
28 Betting game
29 What's not used
30 Places for heros
31 Call off, at Cape Canaveral
32 Cat calls
34 Favorable forecast
37 Referee's demand
41 "We hold ___ truths . . ."
43 Item with a clip or a pin
* 44 Like oranges and lemons
46 Student getting one-on-one help

47 Bed board
48 ___-slaw
49 It's where the heart is
50 Letters before omegas
51 Folk tales and such
52 Work units
53 "Leave it," to a typesetter
56 Summer drink
57 Ice melter

by Nick Grivas

ACROSS

* 1 Hertz competitor
5 Mature
10 Play parts
14 1/500 of the Indianapolis 500
15 Wear away
16 ___ cheese (salad topping)
17 Animal skin
18 Valley ___, Pa.
19 Wild pig
20 Where to get scared
23 Org. with secrets
26 "___ a small world ..."
27 Second of two
28 Still rumpled, as a bed
30 Wineglass features
32 Where to get jarred
34 Insane
37 Child most likely to be spanked
38 ___ de Janeiro
39 Satisfy a hankering
40 Hankering
41 Where to get dizzy
44 Hoity-toity sorts
46 Debit's partner
47 "Little ___ Annie"
50 Decorated war pilot
51 Place to recuperate
52 Gentle alternative to 20-, 32- and 41-Across
56 Shaking chill
57 Computer operators
58 Greasy
62 Full house, e.g.
63 Crème de la crème
64 Quote as an example

65 Bartenders tender them
66 Echolocation
67 Baby goats

DOWN

1 Piece of band equipment
2 Compete
3 Down with the flu
4 Son of Adam and Eve
5 Opponent in an argument
6 Shackles
7 Harbor
8 Perimeter
9 Christmas tree shedding
10 Monastery heads
11 Influence
12 Hardly the prim sort
13 More certain
21 Campaign worker
22 Boars Head product
23 Small compartment
24 Become accustomed (to)
25 Jordan's capital
29 Liable
30 Leaves harbor
31 Gait faster than a walk
33 Test taker's dirty secret
34 Hotel cleaners
35 Just clear of the ocean floor
36 Atlanta-based airline
39 "What ___ Is" (1988 #1 country hit)

41 Languages
42 Plaintiff
43 Carolina ___ (little songster)
44 Rips to bits
45 Opponent's vote
47 University of Nebraska campus site
48 Magnificent
49 Wrinkly fruit
50 Major blood carrier
53 Nobel Peace Prize city
54 Bridle strap
55 Loading area
59 Caesar's three
60 Inc., in Britain
* 61 "You bet!"

by Nancy Kavanaugh

ACROSS

1 Arm bones
6 Tiny swab
10 Rat
14 "___ We All?" (old show tune)
15 With the bow, in music
16 Falls behind
17 Cores
18 Christmas song
19 Money in Milano
20 Witch's phrase, in "Macbeth"
23 Dolt
24 Alliance since 1948: Abbr.
25 Washington's ___ Sound
27 Pep rally cry
30 Tennis champ Ilie
32 Resolutely
35 Bricks measure
36 End of beach season, to many
41 Sheep-ish one
42 Impart, as values
43 Pathetic bumbler
46 Polite turndown
50 Beginners
51 Summer hours in Pa.
53 Baton Rouge sch.
54 Piece of unfinished business
59 It goes to waist
60 Deserving a C
61 Integrates
62 ___ fruit
63 Nutrient in spinach
64 Skirt style
65 Boxer's punching spot
66 Ditto
67 Midterms and finals

DOWN

1 Disheveled
2 Bach piece
3 Partner of cease
4 The "I" in IHOP: Abbr.
5 "___ Long Way to Tipperary"
*6 Lecture follower, briefly
7 Gaits slower than gallops
8 Cake decorator
9 Game on horseback
10 Nearly
11 Follow too closely
12 Consents to
13 Mao ___-tung
21 Wandering
22 Raises
26 Care for
28 Old name for Tokyo
29 ___ Lingus
30 Former Speaker Gingrich
31 Corroded
33 Moist, as a cellar
34 Method: Abbr.
36 For fear that
37 Jackie Gleason catchphrase, with "And"
38 Sleeping bags
39 "Telephone Line" rock grp.
40 Carrier to Amsterdam
44 Troop movement
45 Request
47 French writer ___ de Tocqueville
48 Concurrence
49 Disarranges, as the hair
51 England's ___ Downs
52 Unengaging speaking voice
55 Egyptian fertility goddess
56 "Heartburn" author Ephron
57 Coll. senior's hurdle
*58 Anger, with "up"
59 Hamburger helper?

by Elizabeth C. Gorski

12 LINK LETTERS

ACROSS
1 King with a golden touch
6 Ones wearing knickers
10 Lion's antithesis
14 Sports venue
15 Mideast-based grp.
16 Say for sure
17 Not the sailing sort
19 Quick snack
20 Big bang maker
21 Mine extraction
22 Steamroll
24 Access the Internet, with "on"
25 Postpone
26 Amtrak employee
30 Made a movie
34 Kitchen or den
35 Car until 1957
*37 The "L" in AWOL
38 Spanish museum work
39 Squirrels' homes
41 Diva's song
42 Put on a happy face
44 Confident
45 Obsolescent phone feature
46 "What's ___ you?"
48 Drill instructor, usually
50 They "just want to have fun" in a 1984 song
52 Ruin
53 "The Satanic Verses" author
56 Office seeker, informally
57 Wide of the mark
*60 "L'___ c'est moi": Louis XIV
61 Don Juan, e.g.
64 Cook's seasoning
65 Scientologist ___ Hubbard
66 "The Magic Flute," e.g.
67 In that place, to a whaler
68 Hangup
69 Mary Poppins, e.g.

DOWN
1 Drive-in order
2 Big rug exporter
3 Bumper blemish
4 What's more
5 Place with swinging doors
6 Rounded part
7 N.Y.P.D. alert
8 Mower maker
9 Back of the neck
10 Samuel Gompers, e.g.
11 Tel ___, Israel
12 Dish (out)
13 ___ Fox
18 FedEx notation
23 Moon man Armstrong
24 Stage star
25 "The Cat in the Hat" writer
26 Clean a blackboard
27 Actress Shearer
28 Cry after a catch
29 Supports for specs
31 Newswoman Shriver
32 Poland Spring competitor
33 Handed out, as cards
36 Roll call reply
40 Billy Graham delivery
43 Novelist Bagnold
47 Gives the third degree
49 Cider unit
51 Live's companion
53 Downtime
54 Four Corners state
55 Sweeping story
56 Engine knock
57 Dutch cooker
58 Forest plant
59 Skirmish
62 ___ fault (overmuch)
63 ___-Locka, Fla.

by Gregory E. Paul

ACROSS

1. A property may have one on it
5. Sound of a fall
10. Robed
14. Singer Arnold
15. Piece of garlic
16. Tiptop
17. NATO's first supreme commander
19. Bone parallel to the radius
20. Stage actress Caldwell
21. General Motors line, for short
22. Deodorant type
24. They'll show you the world
26. Done, in Dijon
* 27. Dickens's orphan in "Great Expectations"
28. Tropical plant with a trunklike stem
32. Military capability
35. Stead
36. Polite turndown
37. Russian orbiter
38. Ship navigation aid
39. Uzbekistan's ___ Sea
40. Leafy shelter
42. Massachusetts's nickname
44. H₂0 at 0°
45. Radio amateurs
46. Stranger in a strange land?
50. Win back one's losses
53. Lions and tigers
54. Cause for sudden death
55. "There oughta be ___!"
56. Academic enclave

59. Not yours or theirs
60. Swab the deck again
61. Old piano tunes
62. Ibsen's "___ Gynt"
63. Tickle pink
64. Fortuneteller's opening

DOWN

1. Host Gibbons
2. Numbskull
3. 1950's Ford flop
4. Bill ___, the Science Guy
5. Lug around
6. Walks like a workhorse
7. Areas on weather maps
8. "___ Maria"

9. Wirehair, e.g.
10. It has a big head
11. Hang (around)
12. ___ Domini
13. University V.I.P.
* 18. More meddlesome
23. It's next to nothing
25. Spring event
26. "___ Jacques" (children's song)
28. Bale binder
29. Yeats's land
30. Kind of admiral
31. Woman of habit?
32. ___ song (cheaply)
33. "___, old chap"
34. Leaves out
36. Catch in the act
38. Part of a biblical plague

40. Dracula, for one
41. Genetically related organisms
43. St. Anthony's cross
46. Diviner's deck
47. "___ a dark and stormy night . . ."
48. Start of a long battle
49. Short-winded
50. Wheelchair access
51. Author Wiesel
52. Sugar source
53. Film "sleeper" of 1978
57. Speed: Abbr.
58. "Either you say it ___ will"

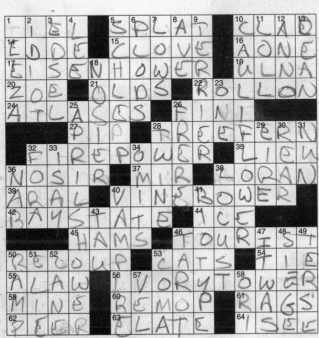

by Dave and Diane Epperson

14 TRANSPORTATION LINES

ACROSS

1 Lump of cream, for example
5 Open a bit
9 Man with a fable
14 Debauchee
15 Wowser
16 Lollipop flavor
17 Really happy, as an angel?
20 ___ dish
21 Al or Tipper
22 When said three times, a 1970 war movie
23 Sault ___ Marie
25 Without principles
27 Really happy, as a kid in March?
33 "Garfield" dog
34 H.S. junior's test
35 Concur
40 Tony-winner Moore
42 Z, on a phone
43 Tailless hoppers
44 Really bother
45 They have their pluses and minuses
47 Currier's partner in lithography
48 Really happy, as a meteorologist?
51 Auto trim
55 Unit of energy
56 Raise, as kids
57 "Two Years Before the ___"
61 "Measure twice, cut once," e.g.
65 Really happy, as a mountaineer?
68 Teatime treat
69 Bulrush, e.g.
70 Remove from a mother's milk
71 Monsieur : Paris :: ___ : Madrid
72 Isn't keeping up with bills
73 Zippo

DOWN

1 Tight hold
2 Sole
3 Bump from office
4 Southernmost city of ancient Palestine
5 Pub order
6 Father of Analytical Psychology
7 Choir voice
8 German industrial region
9 Paleontologist's estimate
10 A Muse
11 Relish
12 "Lohengrin," e.g.
13 Kind of code
18 Ars longa, ___ brevis
19 Miami basketball team
24 Debatable "skill"
26 Vegetarians eschew it (NOT chew it)
27 "Where the heart is"
28 Concept
29 Coated with gold
30 Savory jelly
31 Pope John Paul II's real first name
32 "___ skin off my nose!"
36 Submerging
37 Sitarist Shankar
38 Garden with a snake
39 Start of North Carolina's motto
41 Part of a molecule
46 Take to court
49 Nautilus captain
50 Sketch
51 Angry
52 From now on
53 Betray, in a way
54 Maine college town
58 60's do
59 Fret
60 You, to the Amish
62 Region
63 Happy
64 ___ St. Vincent Millay
66 For each
67 Newsman Bradley et al.

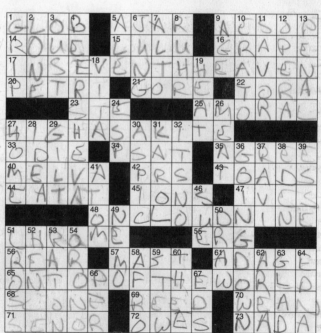

by Richard Hughes

Handwritten margin notes:
ABCDEFGHIJKLMNOPQRSTUVWXYZ
BARS --- S
---- ----
BOND ----
IGHT IGHT
---- ----

ACROSS

1 Important exam
6 Serene
10 Pint sellers
14 Concert site
15 Zone
16 "Make it snappy!"
17 Small salamanders
18 Hussy
19 Pro
20 Command to a sloucher
23 Mutt
25 Mao ___-tung
26 Haunt
27 Nervous
30 Contains
31 Greek theater
32 Stoltz of "Mask"
34 Dog in "Beetle Bailey"
38 Park
41 Dry run
42 Wraps up
43 Losing come-out roll in craps
44 Madrid Mrs.
45 ___ Tunes (cartoon series)
46 Summer attire
50 Hack's workplace
52 Stubborn one
53 Be dead and buried
57 With the bow, in music
58 Na+ and Ca++, e.g.
59 "Cheers" mailman
62 Dressed
63 Authentic
64 Influential member of a tribe
65 Fictional Jane
66 Writer ___ Stanley Gardner
67 Squalid

DOWN

1 Strike out
2 Wrath
3 Bygone cinema bonuses
4 Opposed
5 Remain in good shape
6 Pitches a tent
7 Get up
8 It begins on Ash Wednesday
9 Noted jazz drummer
10 Notre Dame's city
11 Style manual concern
12 Spa
13 Fop's footwear
21 Sport ___ (modern vehicle)
22 Stomach muscles, briefly
23 Take for one's own use
24 Excessive
28 Moron
29 Bearded antelope
30 Top 40 station's play list
32 11,000-foot mount in Europe
33 Pistol, slangily
* 34 Cuatro y cuatro
35 Avert
36 Park features
37 Respects the rules
39 Get worked up?
40 D.D.E.'s command, once
44 Good name for a cook
45 There are 2.2 in a kg.
46 "The final frontier"
47 ___-burly
48 "American Beauty" prize
* 49 ___ Island
50 Ear part
51 Air passenger's request
54 Perpetrator
55 Glitches
56 Vogue competitor
60 Agent from Washington
61 Prepare scrapple, say

by Peter Gordon

ACROSS

1 60's do
5 "Cool!"
9 Tie at a derby?
14 1958 chiller, with "The"
15 Singer Guthrie
16 Melodramatic
17 Baby bear reconnoiterers?
19 President before Polk
20 Person of note?
22 ___ Diavolo (seafood sauce)
23 Puts on an act
26 Conqueror of England, 1066
28 Actress Lena
29 Resorts of sorts
32 Give the heave-ho
33 Cowpoke competitions
36 Klingons and Vulcans
38 Coming-out party?
39 Baby fox carriers?
41 Form filer, for short
44 Platforms
*46 Lords and ladies
48 Dundee denizen
50 Charlie Brown expletive
52 Security concern
53 Player who's good with a bat
55 Bishops' subordinates
58 German cry
59 B-52, e.g.
62 Caterpillar competitor
64 Baby bird vegetables?
68 Boo-boo
69 Computer clickers

70 Oscar-winner Kazan
71 Medicine measures
72 Said "not guilty," e.g.
73 It's in a pickle

DOWN

1 "N.Y.P.D. Blue" network
2 Winter woe
3 Rip off
4 Really awful
5 One of the Judds
6 Blows one's top
7 Kind of clef
8 Not sleep peacefully
9 Houston player
10 Sauce source
11 Baby moose movers?

12 Met productions
13 Tough boss to work for
18 Comedian Bill, informally
21 Naval Academy grad
23 Escort company
24 Mother Nature's burn balm
25 Baby goat siblings?
27 "Apollo 13" director Howard
30 Blue Ribbon maker
31 In the style of
34 Green-lights
35 Environmentalists' club name
*37 That, to Tomás
40 Caroler's syllable

42 Marsh material
43 Questions
45 ___ Industries (defense contractor)
47 Censored
48 Protected from the sun
49 "O tempora! O mores!" orator
51 Piece together, as tape
54 Water servers
56 Sped
57 Press coverage
60 Dudley Do-Right's org.
61 Pop singer Collins
63 Seafood delicacy
65 Actor Wallach
66 Be laid up
67 Mule of song

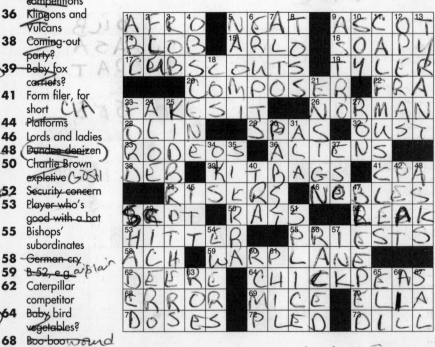

by Nancy Salomon

ACROSS

1 In the thick of
5 Fallings-out
10 Nose (out)
14 Chauffeur's spot
15 Ahead of the game
16 In need of patching
17 ___ uproar
18 Food from heaven
19 Old-time oath
20 They're loaded
23 Dan Aykroyd's old show, briefly
24 "What a good boy ___!"
25 Ground-breakers?
26 French composer Erik
28 Bluegrass strings
30 They're loaded
32 Native Alaskan
33 Sound like a siren
35 Uno + dos
* 36 Possible title for this puzzle
39 Telegram punctuation
42 Words from Wordsworth
43 More boorish
47 They're loaded
49 Per ___ income
50 Some tournaments
51 Garr of "Mr. Mom"
53 Floral ring
54 PBS benefactor
55 They're loaded
59 Poet ___ St. Vincent Millay
61 Earth that's "firma"
62 ___ Hotels (luxury chain)
63 Botch

64 Stream
65 Mideast sultanate
66 Humane org.
67 Pays attention to
68 Good buds

DOWN

1 "Arabian Nights" hero
2 Barely adequate
3 Use the mind's eye
4 Slips into
5 Ladies' men
6 Really dumb
7 ___ for oneself (goes it alone)
8 The sound of music
9 Practice in the ring
10 Ram's ma'am
11 Part of Canis Major
12 Rock for a monument
13 Nonstop
21 ID item
22 Concorde, e.g.
27 Goes on the fritz
29 Attack
30 Whopper juniors?
31 Pie ___ mode
33 Ties the knot with
34 Admiral's affirmative
37 Alternative to smoking
38 Last Supper cup
39 Those who shouldn't live in glass houses?
* 40 Prepared, as a memo

41 Sea-dwelling
44 Thorny problem
45 Nonstop
46 Cereal fruit
48 City in Kyrgyzstan
49 Frog-sounds
51 Wee hour
52 Slipped up
56 Rash reaction?
57 Richard of "Pretty Woman"
58 Cloverleaf feature
60 Santa ___ winds

by Harvey Estes and Nancy Salomon

18 FIELD STRIP

REN_TO_ S_ACKS
S___WN T_SH

ACROSS

1 Bit of parsley
6 Go crazy, slangily
10 "Woe is me!"
14 Historical 1960 John Wayne film, with "The"
15 Bit
16 Hardly the life of the party
17 Headline about lightning hitting a landfill?
19 1996 also-ran
20 Psychic's claim
21 See 2-Down
22 Get, as an idea
24 Gets ore
26 Jiffy
27 Child punishment tool?
33 Afrikaners
34 "Cool!"
35 Noted 1964 convert to Islam
36 Character
37 Offspring
39 Assist a writer
40 The Braves, on scoreboards
41 Aberdeen native
42 First sign of spring
43 What the Little Engine That Could experienced?
47 Leader in a 1972 summit meeting with Nixon
48 Scarlett's third
49 Garden pavilions
53 Faulkner's "___ Lay Dying"
54 Pub quaff
57 Skating jump
58 Student who plays hooky at noon?
61 Pro or con

62 Actor Estrada
63 Bale binder
64 "Hey!"
65 TV rooms
66 Ice cream drinks

DOWN

1 Marquis de ___
2 Sign used in a 21-Across
3 Alternative to steps
4 Mischief-maker
5 Spreads rumors
6 Less flexible
7 "Mambo No. 5" singer ___ Bega
8 Yen
9 Islamabad's country
10 Take into a flying saucer, say

11 Roller coaster part
12 Folk singer Guthrie
13 Viewed
18 Bluefin, e.g.
23 New driver's hurdle
24 Simple
25 Gramm or Grams
27 Wisdom
28 "You there?"
29 Right from the factory
30 r's, in geometry
31 Not of this world
32 They may be bottomless
33 Brie-a-___
37 Taught
38 Nanki-___ of "The Mikado"

39 Part of Q.E.D.
41 Wound cover
42 Drawers
44 Egg dish
45 Not the finest homes
46 Musician John
49 [You don't mean THAT!]
50 Allies' foe
51 Last letters, in England
52 Positive
54 Like a desert
55 Actress Turner
56 Snake ___ (60-Down)
59 Writer Anaïs
60 See 56 Down

by Tyler Hinman

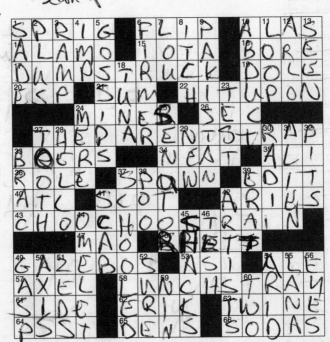

ACROSS

1 Place for a fire
5 Oklahoma's state tree
11 Hot resort? SPA
14 Water for Juan
15 May who directed "Ishtar"
16 Middle X of X-X-X
17 It's closed for fighting
18 Initial consideration
20 Powers that be
22 Law, in Lyon /ex
23 Church recess
24 It sweeps across the face £ £ _ £ han role
27 Requiring sudden death TIED
28 Amateur sports org.
29 Ecclesiastical gathering
31 Buckeyes' sch.
34 Ribosomal __
36 __ Rock (Australian tourist site)
39 Possible title for this puzzle
44 Disney theme park
45 Singing cowboy Ritter
46 Wee one KID
47 Windblown soil
50 "__ the Wild Wind" (DeMille movie) RIDE
53 Do library research
55 Unindustrialized
60 Actor Jannings
61 It comes with a charge
62 Flight segment
63 Headquarters

67 Thomas __ Edison
68 Had dinner
69 Flatware factory worker
70 Boo-boo
71 Hospital unit
72 Somebody
73 London's __ Park

DOWN

1 Parisian sidewalk sights
2 Sprightly
3 "The __ of the spheres"
4 George C. Scott's Oscar-winning role
5 Whistle blower
6 Yalie
7 "Our Gang" girl
* 8 Buffalo Bill's targets: Var.
9 Piglike
10 Belle of the ball
* 11 Maximally dense
12 Antiquated
13 Longed (for)
19 Singer Jackson
21 Business letter abbr.
25 "Shucks!"
26 Suspend
30 Make a collar
31 Pay dirt
32 Have dinner
33 Like some airport luggage
35 Part of "D.A.": Abbr. ATY
37 Antique auto
38 Speedy flier
40 Gray matter

41 Suffix with Canaan
42 Mannheim mister
43 Crossed (out)
48 Suppress
49 Yom Kippur horn
51 Cornball comebacks
52 Soap ingredient
53 Starting-over place
54 Ham it up
56 Everything __ place
57 Good news on Wall Street
58 More than miffed IRKED
59 Arrange gracefully
64 Antonym: Abbr.
65 Top of the corp. ladder
66 Seabird

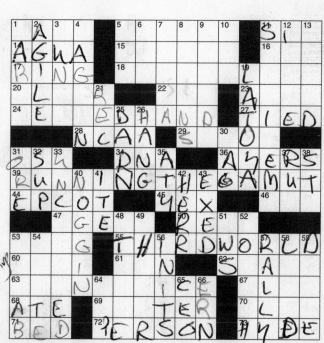

by Nick Grivas and Nancy Salomon

20 LESS IS MORE

ACROSS

1 Game of kings and queens
6 Show snide satisfaction
11 Act like
14 Artificial jewelry
15 Winchester, for one
16 Lobster ___ Diavolo
17 Pounce on some mariners' gear
19 In favor of
20 Gusto
21 Off the leash
23 Where Woodstock can be found
27 Used a teaspoon
29 Changes
30 Interlaced
31 Card catalogue listing
32 Fetch
33 Pompous person
36 List ender
37 Really bad
38 "___ first you don't . . ."
39 Kind of room
40 Bowwow
41 Hacienda brick
42 Black belt activity
44 Capital of South Dakota
45 Military school
* 47 Celebrated Mardi Gras, in a way
48 ___ 6
49 Maintained
50 Victoria's Secret purchase
51 Validate, businesswise
58 Resinous substance
59 Ruin of a statue, perhaps
60 Tennessee footballer
61 Wapiti
62 Live
63 Sonneteer's Muse

DOWN

1 I.R.S. job applicant, maybe
2 Owns
3 Tee preceder
4 Sched. locale
5 Confiscation
6 Hawaiian skirt material
7 Top 10, e.g.
8 "Birth ___ Nation"
9 Actress MacGraw
10 Revelatory
11 Be able to buy some wheels
12 Simple writing
13 Like a ewer
18 "___ Fall in Love"
22 Refinable rock
23 Object of a Latin prayer
24 Cream of the crop
25 Start hammering
26 Carter of sitcoms
27 Make a rustling sound
28 Pint-sized
30 Armistice
32 Spoils of war
34 Buffalo hockey player
35 Spirited horse
37 Rich soil
38 Concept
40 Church dignitary
41 When a show is broadcast
43 Citrus drink
44 It may be read
45 Stroll
46 Reef material
47 Candidate of 1992 and '96
49 Sound like a snake
52 CBS competitor
53 Night that "Miami Vice" was on: Abbr.
54 Christmas buy
55 Call ___ day
56 Betrayer
* 57 L-P filler

by Richard Silvestri

ACROSS

1 Poker variation
* 5 Sources of delight
* 9 Bashful, e.g.
14 Improve, as one's skills
15 Sector
16 Contest in the West
17 Milo's pal, in a 1989 film
18 Word after body or grand
19 Avoid answering
20 "While I'm away on vacation, would you ___ . . .?"
23 Object of an old French cheer
24 Gives in to gravity
25 Quick-witted
28 Over there, poetically
30 Surface sheen
32 Battering device
35 "And ___ . . .?"
38 Designer Cassini
40 Teeny
41 One of two on a brig
42 "And ___ . . .?"
47 Place to do the samba
48 Editor/suffragist Bloomer
49 Begin a hand
51 Neither's partner
52 Nudge forward
55 Streetcars
58 "And ___?"
61 Stick that's waved
64 Plane prefix
65 Old TV clown
66 Glorify
67 Alka-Seltzer jingle starter
68 Started a gunfight

69 Tropical lizard
70 Political doctrines
71 Capitol Hill worker

DOWN

1 Third place
2 Wreck beyond recognition
3 Bring together
4 Catch sight of
5 Incense scent
6 Paris airport
7 Informal affirmatives
8 Pago Pago's place
9 Put on one's Sunday best
10 Made a tapestry
11 Cavity fillers' org.
12 Like a sunset

13 Any Hatfield, to a McCoy
21 Foot that goes clop
22 Hideous
* 25 How some stocks sell
26 Coke competitor
27 "___ Remember" (1960 song)
29 Like a morning meadow
31 Addition solution
32 Mr. Bean portrayer Atkinson
33 Crockett's last stand
34 Cabbie's counter
36 Neighbor of Md.
37 Honey drink
39 Hairstyling goop

43 Attack verbally
44 Painter Chagall
45 Does a swab's job
46 Not (a one)
50 Kappa follower
53 Giraffelike beast
54 Combats of honor
56 New Zealand native
57 Measured, with "up"
58 Tyler and Taylor's go-between
59 Place for a king and queen
60 1993 Emmy winner Chad
61 Dog command
62 Chopper
63 Middle X or O

by Patrick Jordan

FULL OF GRACE

ACROSS

* 1 "Macbeth" quintet
5 Distort
9 Place for a mirrored ball
14 Smith Brothers unit
15 Actress Spelling
16 Poland Spring competitor
17 Object of a classic pursuit
19 43-Across division
20 Rice University mascot
21 The life of __
22 Tee off
23 S. & L. offerings
24 Lupino of "High Sierra"
25 Elvis or Fabian, once
26 Childbirth
31 Kind of wool or drum
34 Some drafts
35 Rocky pinnacle
36 Didn't give way
37 Eric Clapton classic
39 Jim-dandy
40 Before, to Burns
41 Haughty pose
42 Tack on
43 Hellish literary work
47 Aardvark's meal
48 Brian of Roxy Music
49 Shriver of tennis
52 Photo finish
54 Family name at Indy
56 In need of salting, perhaps
57 Little green man
58 You can't touch this
60 Embellish
61 Deer sir
62 Gumbo ingredient
63 Heavenly gift
64 __-poly
65 Part of MOMA's address

DOWN

1 Kind of committee
2 Jam-pack
3 Trucker's expense
4 Le Carré character
5 Big step
6 Eucalyptus-eating animals
7 Iroquoian Indian
8 Cunning
9 The Roaring 20's and others
10 Chekhov's first play
11 Playing card without a match
12 Blanchett of "Elizabeth"
13 __ close to schedule
18 Give the third degree
25 Brainstorm
26 Fourposter, e.g.
27 Final authority
28 Wright wing?
29 Poor dog's portion
30 "Jurassic Park" beast, for short
31 Get rid of
32 Hatcher of "Lois & Clark"
33 One mile, for Denver
37 Golf positions
38 Compass creation
39 "__ Given Sunday"
41 One of a bug's pair
42 Be nuts over
44 Trainee or detainee
45 Peyote
46 The "E" in $E = mc^2$
49 Hard to please
50 Squirreled-away item
51 Sinatra classic
52 Hat-tipper's word
* 53 "Betsy's Wedding" star
54 The Beatles' "Back in the __"
55 Cold war winner
59 Mafia figure

by Randall J. Hartman

ACROSS
1 Two smackers?
5 "___ la Douce"
9 Is eliminated from competition
14 Yearn (for)
15 Contemptible one
16 Take over
17 Mason's wedge
18 Italian lake
19 Hawaiian party site
20 1932 novel of crime and race by 40-Across
23 British biscuit
25 Berlin bar need
26 One-on-one sport
27 From a personal standpoint
30 Slump
32 Genesis victim
33 Symbol of sturdiness
35 Mind terribly
40 See 20- and 57-Across
43 Hung around
44 ___-de-sac
45 Cutting part
46 Q-U connection
48 Kind of film
50 It may react with an acid
54 Swiss canton
56 Fish that's split for cooking
57 Fictional county, locale of 20-Across
61 Hearty breakfast dish
62 MOMA artist
63 "Bus Stop" playwright
66 Cheri of "Saturday Night Live"
67 Dash
68 Hoops tournament org.
69 Bells the cat
70 "Auld Lang ___"
71 Dinero

DOWN
1 ___ Vegas
2 German pronoun
3 In myth she was changed into a nightingale
4 From the very beginning
5 Dermatologist's concern
6 Kind of vegetable
7 Ike's mate
8 Poster boy
9 Lollapalooza
10 ___ orange
11 Dawn
12 Delete
13 Maliciousness
21 Washington, e.g.: Abbr.
22 Usually
23 Bandleader Artie and others
24 Biblical length
28 Packs a lot in
29 Edible 6-Down
31 Hair goop
34 Popular fast-food chain
36 Outlining
37 Marathoner's trait
38 The "N" of U.N.C.F.
39 Unable to escape
41 Ending with cash or bombard
42 "___ Wiedersehen"
47 Swaps
49 Nile reptile
50 "I swear . . . !"
51 Feeder of the body's organs
52 Winter sight at Tahoe
53 ___ nous
55 Where Soave comes from
58 Yard sale tag
59 Ladd or Alda
60 Soave, e.g.
64 Guy's honey
65 "Dig in!"

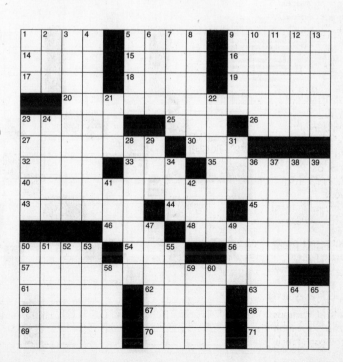

by Joy L. Wouk

ACROSS

1. ___ Lee cakes
5. Nifty
9. Places for plaques
14. Sit (down)
15. "This round's ___"
16. Duck
17. Charitable donations
18. Brain wave
19. Moses' mount
20. John Denver sang it in 1975
23. French sea
24. "___ out!" (ump's call)
25. Dis's opposite
26. School zone caution
28. Posture problem
30. Piercing places
32. Shakespeare's was "mortal"
33. Steamed (up)
35. Boozer
36. Make ___ dash for
37. Gwen Verdon sang it in 1966
41. "Out with it!"
42. Nod from offstage, maybe
43. Toupee, slangily
44. Inn inventory
45. Lip service?
47. Kind of list
51. Word before and after "oh"
52. Hobbyist's place
53. "Take out the trash," repeatedly
55. Xmas time: Abbr.
56. Elvis Presley sang it in 1962
60. Calf-length skirts
61. Cuddly "Return of the Jedi" creature
* 62. Pierce player on "M*A*S*H"
63. In a rut
64. Small, medium or large
65. Like the diver's end of the pool
66. Illicit cab
67. Act the worrywart
68. Tacks on

DOWN

1. Jerks
2. Completely off-base
3. The Joker portrayer Cesar
4. Church alcove
5. Boom or zoom
6. Stand the test of time
* 7. U.S.A. part: Abbr.
8. Pendant gem shape
9. "Fuzzy Wuzzy ___ fuzzy"
10. Gung-ho
11. Wanting company
12. 1997 Jim Carrey comedy
13. Reagan's long-range plan?: Abbr.
21. Laid-back
22. Break time
27. Vintage
29. "But of course!"
31. Silly sorts
32. Bum off of
34. Heart
37. Boisterous fun
38. Tied
39. Brand in a bar
40. Elbow
41. Looker's leg
46. Catch some Z's
48. Mixed up
49. Had to have
50. Tidbits for Fido
52. Somewhat dark
54. Cockeyed
57. Nervous twitches
58. Simple Simon
59. Zapata's "zip"
60. Flavor enhancer, briefly

by Nancy Salomon and Sherry O. Blackard

ACROSS

1 "You missed a ___!"
5 Hilo hello
10 Summer place
14 Heather Headley title role on Broadway
15 Lions' locks
16 Concluded
17 2000 runner
19 Alternative to hot pants
20 Go astray
21 They're on tap in taprooms
22 Coats with gold
23 Stir up
24 Humor that's not funny
26 Classic Chevy
29 Broadway aunt
30 ___ dog (backwoods animal)
31 Game for the asocial
36 What 55-Across is to 17-Across
39 Toppled, in a way
40 Reply to the Little Red Hen
41 "Off with you!"
42 Frank
44 Part of a freight train
48 ___ on (orders to attack)
49 Ill-gotten gains
50 Prego competitor
51 Part of a litter
54 Sparkling wine center
55 See 36-Across
58 Rung
59 Restaurateur of song
60 Brezhnev's land
61 Famous alter ego
62 Got smart, with "up"
63 Ravioli filler

DOWN

1 Solomon
2 Jetty
3 Locker room emanation
4 Driveway material
5 Aviator Earhart
6 RCA or Columbia
7 Burden
8 "___ a Rebel" (1962 #1 hit)
9 Straight-grained wood
10 Chris Rock, for one
11 1950's Indians All-Star Bobby
12 Darns
13 Rainbow maker
18 Famous Dartmoor facility
22 Garbo of "Anna Christie"
23 Dude's place?
24 First course, maybe
25 Notorious Idi
26 Like shrimp during shipping
27 Infiltrator
28 Langston Hughes, e.g.
29 Dollars and Deutsche marks
31 Echo analyzer
32 Choreographer de Mille
33 Monopoly token
34 5¢/gallon, e.g.
35 Head of state in Kuwait
37 Vestige
38 Where Red Delicious apples originated
* 42 Like a London jurist
43 Some hosp. rooms
44 Jiffy
45 Robust
46 Functioned
47 Rubbish
48 50-Across, e.g.
50 McGwire stats
51 Sit for a photograph
52 ___ Minor
* 53 Overly familiar, maybe
55 Hee's follower
56 Whitney of gin fame
57 Ruin, with "up"

by Ed Early

ACROSS

1 On the ocean
6 Andy's radio partner
10 Dish that sticks to your ribs
14 Hunky-dory
15 1993 film in which Kevin Kline played the president
16 Chair-raising experience?
17 Miami sights
18 Kind of hygiene
19 Singer Redding
20 Don Shula or Knute Rockne
23 "___ Misérables"
25 Doc for a boxer
26 Expenditure
27 Single-celled protozoa
30 Place to have a pint
*31 Less common
32 Mickey's creator
34 Comics canine
38 Scold severely
41 Cheers for banderilleros
42 Bitter drinks
43 Seashore
44 Insect in a colony
45 Goodness
46 On the train
50 Luau food
52 "___ Haw"
53 Rosa Parks Day
57 Bread spread
58 "Oh, that'll happen!"
59 Heart outlet
62 Blueprint
63 Intent look
64 Plane seating division (and the key to this puzzle's theme)

*65 Change for a twenty
66 Sought damages
67 Part of a ruble

DOWN

1 Killer snake
2 U.S. Airways competitor
3 Like buffet restaurants
4 Ticklish doll guy
5 In addition
6 Building brick
7 French radical murdered in his bathtub
8 White House office shape
9 Events with no empty seats
10 Make a film
11 Horribly wreck
12 "Fear of Flying" writer Jong
13 Wishy-___
21 Attachments to VCR's
22 Chicago athlete
23 Key ___
24 Correspondence that may come with attachments
28 Apiary residents
29 High school elective
30 In addition
32 Whip mark
33 Homer Simpson's dad
34 ___ about (approximately)
35 Ira Levin play
36 Matter of dispute
37 Cosmetician Lauder
39 Lipstick holders
40 Here, in France
44 Radius's place
45 The Henry who founded the Tudor line
46 Take in, as a stray cat
47 "Beauty and the Beast" beauty
48 Indian ___
49 Ages and ages
50 Trophy
51 Killed, slangily
54 Rebecca and Isaac's eldest
55 Spice holder
56 Fly without a co-pilot
60 Mao ___-tung
61 Interview

by Peter Gordon

ACROSS

1 ". . . and carry ___ stick"
5 Concerning
9 With 69-Across, locales for this puzzle's theme
*14 Mugger repellent
*15 Ensure the failure of
16 Divination deck
17 "Who ___?" (knock response)
18 History test answer
19 Make giddy with delight
20 "Kitty Foyle" Oscar winner
23 Vice president with a "Jr." in his name
24 Brouhaha
25 Over: Fr.
28 ___ Spumante
31 Baby bottle topper
33 U.N.C. is in it
36 Word from the wise
38 Where birds fly in the fall
41 What "it" plays
42 Pittsburgh product
43 Brown-nose
46 A.M.A. members
47 "Ripe" stage of life
48 Jacob's twin
50 6-pointers
51 Altar avowal
53 Dishes
58 TV staple since 1969
61 Have dinner at home
64 Seasoned sailor
65 57-Down request
66 Draw ___ in the sand
67 Notion
68 About 30% of the earth's land
69 See 9-Across
70 Burn with a branding iron
71 Be "it"

DOWN

1 Old computer
2 Actor Rathbone
3 Cake topper
4 Very beginning
5 State of the Union, e.g.
6 Fly high
7 Dog in Oz
8 Alpha's opposite
9 Some bodybuilders' body builders
10 Cronies
11 Lyricist Gershwin
12 Barracks bed
13 Summer on the Seine
21 Piece of history
22 1999–2000 "Dame" on Broadway
25 Looked in (on)
*26 Stress symptom, they say
27 Projection booth items
29 "Later!"
30 "___ at the office"
32 Cpl.'s inferior
33 Yachtsman's neckwear
34 Was capable of
35 Half of Miss Muffet's dish
37 Capital I's
39 ___-la-la
40 Cleanliness regimens
44 Agents from D.C.
45 Eminem, e.g.
49 Nth deg.
52 Caravan's spot
54 Rich tapestry
55 Flirt with
56 Goosebump-raising
57 The turf in "surf and turf"
58 Wash-up spot
59 Fabricated
60 Philosopher Zeno of ___
61 Swab target
62 In the style of
63 Personal quirk

by Chris Sallade

ACROSS

1 Door frame upright
5 Muslim's journey
9 Mosque officials
14 Kind of arguments
15 "Typee" sequel
16 KwaZulu-___ province, South Africa
17 Airport/hotel connection
18 Take to ___ (reprimand)
19 Sales clerk's minimum
20 Faces up to expected hardship
23 Tappan ___ Bridge
24 Le ___ Soleil (Louis XIV)
25 Soapmaking need
26 Snake with a nasty bite
29 Reindeer herder
32 Promgoers: Abbr.
34 Emotes
40 Muscle quality
41 Prefix with center
42 1997 Peter Fonda title role
43 Falls for a scam
48 Kipling novel
49 Shirt brand
* 50 Start of the 16th century
51 Ex of Frank and Artie
54 Singer Zadora
56 Moon vehicle
58 Takes in recent events
64 Sicily's "kicker"
65 Act on, as advice
66 Gung-ho quality
68 Constellation with a belt
69 Linen color
70 "Beetle Bailey" boob
71 Part of SST
72 Carpentry class
73 Thumbs-up

DOWN

1 Scribble
2 Riyadh resident
3 Shin-covering skirt
4 Football charge
5 Uncomfortable position
6 Latin 101 verb
7 Kid
8 Ace topper
9 Ask
10 Stake-driving hammer
11 Bikini, for one
12 Brit's buddy
13 Candidate list
21 Snakelike swimmers
22 Pear variety
26 "Hamlet" has five
27 Come in third
28 Elizabeth of "La Bamba"
30 "That was close!"
31 RC competitor
33 Social rebuff
35 "Champagne music" maestro
36 Therapeutic kind of bath
37 Western film actor Jack
* 38 Nevada Sen. Harry
39 Himalayan legend
44 Not really sing
45 Leave out
46 Hid from pursuers
47 First place?
51 "So long"
52 In ___ fertilization
53 Once more
55 Contents of some urns
57 Certain soprano
59 "The Time Machine" people
60 Kind of support
61 Decorated cop, say
62 Half a fortnight
63 "___ Smile" (Hall & Oates hit)
67 Moviedom's Myrna

by Bill Zais

ACROSS

1 Trifle
7 Scenery spoiler
11 "Kapow!"
14 Pleistocene Epoch, familiarly
15 Come into view
16 Skilled horseman of the Old West
17 Roads to wedded bliss?
19 Sign of success
20 Any old town
21 Grand party
22 End of 14-Across
23 Timeline sections *
25 Beach accessory
28 Prenuptial nerves?
32 See 63-Across
33 Nix from Nixon, e.g.
34 Bossy boss
36 Artist Rousseau
38 Give it ___
40 Stake
41 Director's cry
43 Ancient Andean
45 Altdorf's canton
46 Snort of a confirmed bachelor?
49 Quality camera
50 Word processing command
* 51 It may be critical
53 Campus marchers: Abbr.
55 The last Mrs. Chaplin
59 Latin trio leader
60 Advice to a wannabe princess?
63 With 32-Across, a 1983 Lionel Richie hit
64 Horace tome
65 "Wait Till the Sun Shines" girl
66 Nile reptile
67 Stag, in a way
68 Renders unyielding

DOWN

1 The "Gee" in Bee Gees
2 Hose hue
3 Small dam
4 Potato peeler, e.g.
5 Turkish honorific
6 Prosperity
7 Part of a farm feeder
8 Some church music *
9 "That feels good!"
10 A.L. or N.L. V.I.P.'s
11 Amateurish
12 Razor brand
13 Siamese-speak
18 100 centimos
22 Prefix with -zene
24 It has full pockets
26 Baseball's Master Melvin
27 Disobedient
28 Betel palm
29 Vegetarian protein source
30 Stray from the herd
31 Quite a dummy
32 "That's it!"
35 Prefix with athlete
37 Gets promoted
39 Taxi sign
42 Japanese computer giant
44 Things people do to get their kicks?
47 Speed (along)
48 Noggin
51 Poet Angelou
52 Pop singer Tori
54 About
56 Heraldic border
57 Diamond of music
58 Bowls over
60 Calendar pages: Abbr.
61 Big deal
62 Bottom line

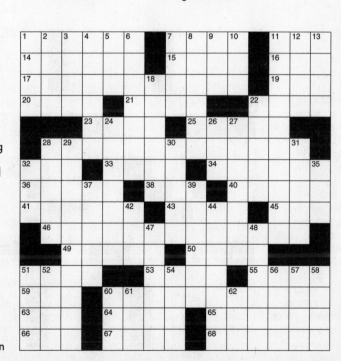

by Nancy Salomon and Sherry O. Blackard

ACROSS

1 Verbal assault
5 Verbal break-in
9 Way around Paris
14 Offer as proof
15 Stuff to be crunched
16 Hatch on the Hill
17 Book after Joel
18 Old Dodge
19 Plain speaking
* 20 Himalayan aviation board?
23 Filled the bill, perhaps
24 November honoree
25 Freshest stories?
34 Bert's buddy
* 35 Third-smallest of nine
36 Maker or breaker lead-in
37 Tour dates
38 Bugs Bunny and others
40 Merlin, e.g.
41 Whiz
42 On toast, at a diner
43 Readied the bow
44 Closeup of royal displeasure?
48 Sch. in Troy, N.Y.
49 "Is that so!"
50 Indiana team hijinks summary?
59 Storming
60 Beethoven's birthplace
61 RC, e.g.
62 Frasier's brother
63 Be an omen of
64 Homeboy's place
65 Exasperates
66 Apple color enhancer
67 Numbered work

DOWN

1 Digitize, in a way
2 Lawn application
3 Resting on
4 ___ Verde National Park
5 Takes on
6 Dogpatch, for one
7 Sicilian peak
8 It may be bounding
9 Rug rats
10 Slips
11 Suffix in nuclear physics
12 Court order?
13 Scott Turow's first book
21 Eleventh-hour
22 Middle of a noted Cubs trio
25 Over 21, perhaps
26 Writer Jong
27 Reason for the silent treatment
28 Family girl
29 In with
30 PC linkup
31 Andean wool source
32 Hot to trot
33 Bjorn Borg, for one
38 Like inner tubes
39 Be in the red
40 N.L. Central team, on scoreboards
42 Lower
43 Golden finish?
45 Grimm heroine
46 Chairman's paper
47 "My Fair Lady" lyricist
50 Engine sound
51 Part of a score, maybe
52 "Tails," e.g.
53 "SOS" pop group
54 Summer hangout
55 Sonar's principle
56 Group enterprise
57 Baseball family name
58 Pew parts

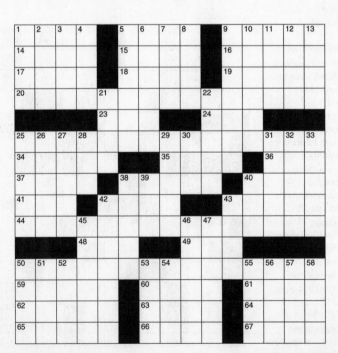

by Greg Staples

ACROSS

1 Diploma word
4 Gives the double-O
9 Hockey's Morenz
14 ___ roll
15 See 8-Down
16 Intercontinental range
17 Lennox Lewis org. *
18 Easy golf shot
19 Infamous motel owner
20 It begins with H
23 Jack of "Rio Lobo"
24 Start of a MacArthur quote
25 They have Xings
28 Ritardando undoer
30 Howard of "Gone With the Wind"
32 Snigglers
36 Barfly's binge
37 "Sic semper tyrannis!" crier
42 Harem rooms
43 1976 uprising site
44 Balm of ___ (fragrant resin)
47 "The Bourne Identity" author
51 ___-Cone
52 Like a virgin?
56 New Rochelle college
57 Classic detection device
60 TV host Gibbons
62 Part of a magician's incantation
63 Owns
64 Kind of circle
65 Rich dessert
66 Havana residue
67 Like Dennis the Menace

68 Make ___ at
69 Juan Carlos, e.g.

DOWN

1 Black-eyed legume
2 Release, in a way
3 Gordon of "Oklahoma!"
4 Prefix with -pod
5 Showy irises
6 ___ lazuli
7 Segal or Fromm
8 With 15-Across, a California county
9 Telescope name
10 Like the Sabin vaccine
11 Crushing defeat
12 ___ de France
13 Non-P.C. suffix

21 Vast
22 Set or wet preceder
26 Quite a comedy
27 Genesis son
29 Nave bench
31 Substituted (for)
33 U.S. Open champ in '94 and '97
34 MGM rival, once
35 Wrap (up)
37 Uses a treadmill, maybe
38 Valhalla V.I.P.
39 Column 7A of the 20-Across
40 Good news for theater owners
41 Heat quantity meas.
45 It's for the birds

46 B.S., e.g.
48 Mandrake's assistant
49 Disquiet
50 Soft and wet
53 Nasal dividers
54 Cavalry unit
55 Capital of Ghana
58 O.T. book before Daniel
59 Takes advantage of
60 Modern piercing site
* 61 Ethyl ending

by Randy Sowell

ACROSS
1 Dolt
5 Unit of capacitance
10 Recover
14 Do road work
15 Certain teasing
16 Org. concerned with due process
17 It may be a double in the Olympics
18 Comedian Robert
19 Nickname for a 6-foot 140-pounder, say
20 It's part of growing up
23 Bering ___: Abbr.
25 This should always be 24-Down
26 Immobilizer
27 Carolina fliers
* 31 Sound
32 Makeshift rodeo seating
33 Ninnies
34 Big success
35 African capital
40 Center of many an orbit
41 Uproar
42 Report boastfully
48 It makes a lot of scents
49 Model Carol
50 Pen
51 Al Kaline and Roberto Clemente
55 Pay to play
56 Basket fiber
57 Help, as a prankster
60 Wrest (from)
61 Overindulges
62 PBS science series
63 Nose (out)
64 Marriott rival
65 The original Lola, in "Damn Yankees"

DOWN
1 Busy worker in Apr.
2 Loose
3 Nullify
4 Supermarket feature
5 Ad-lib
6 Poise
7 Water hazard
8 Give it ___ (swing hard)
9 The 60's Celtics, e.g.
* 10 Getting through a busy toll plaza, e.g.
11 Bakery treat
12 Adjusts, as tires
13 "Network" director
21 Western lake
22 Geom. solid
23 Loot
24 See 25-Across
28 Enlisted men
29 Safari sight
30 ___ Chex
34 "What's that?"
35 ___ worse than death
36 Chicago pro
37 Medieval weapon
38 Not a close game
39 Bohemian
40 Having an "I" problem?
42 Complained
43 Shabby
44 Belong
45 Asian holiday
46 Croquet need
47 Firstborn
48 Pack securely
52 Ray Charles's "What'd ___"
53 Singer James
54 Telephoned
58 Threshold
59 Thrash

by Alan Arbesfeld

ACROSS

1 Ready
5 Vast extents
*10 Break in relations
*14 Cassowary cousins
15 Look for
16 Sneaking suspicion
17 Humor in its verse possible form?
19 Showy flower, for short
20 Basket twigs
21 Poetic palindrome
22 Wife of Zeus
23 Dernier ___
24 Prerevolutionary state
26 Parts of geometry calculations
27 Edit comedy scripts?
31 Scale member
32 Summon, in a way
33 City ESE of Bombay
34 Plowed land
36 It creates drafts
38 Disney's middle name
39 Plummet's opposite
40 ___ Missouri
41 Comedy writing?
44 "___ China" policy
45 Full-service components?
46 Gaelic "Gee!"
47 Petit four finisher
50 When it's broken, that's good
51 Wedding sites
54 Move like molasses
55 Joke postscripts?
57 Lean and sinewy
58 Wool source

59 Blow off steam
60 Word for Yorick
61 Badlands formations
62 Son of Seth

DOWN

1 Defaulter's loss
2 Stern competitor
3 Cure for sick jokes?
4 Fragrant compounds
5 Farm mothers
6 Farm mother
7 Totally gone
8 Coyote State capital
9 "Sophie's Choice" Oscar winner
10 "Stat!"
11 Like some rumors
12 Four Freedoms subject
*13 "Behold!"
*18 Uris hero
24 1997 Fonda role
25 Fab
26 W.W. I French soldier
27 Seek spare change
28 Witticism capital?
29 "Ocupado"
30 Where cures are discovered
31 Stage
32 ___ metabolism
35 Eel look-alikes
36 ___ de Bologne (park west of Paris)
37 Grammy category

39 Hillary supporters
42 Flamethrower fuel
43 Bread or butter
44 Pianist's span
46 Getting on
47 Caucus state
48 Slinky, basically
49 Browning's "Rabbi Ben ___"
51 Literary collections
52 City near Sparks
53 Tu-144 and others
56 Actress Thurman

by William A. Ballard

GOT A CLUE?

ACROSS

* 1 "Later, dude!"
6 Bowlful for Bowser
10 Lefts from Louis
14 Swashbuckling Flynn
15 Long bath
16 Sometimes-twisted snack
17 Hamper
18 News agency founded in 1918
19 Troy Aikman's alma mater
20 Sound of disapproval
21 "Ver-r-rry funny!"
24 Burt's "The Killers" co-star
25 Female hog
26 Batting avg., e.g.
29 Father Flanagan's group, today
35 The Earps, e.g.
37 In addition
38 Aware of
39 To pieces
40 Shirt part
41 Show fear
42 Part of the uvea
43 "What ___, chopped liver?"
44 Improvise
45 1980's antidrug campaigner
48 Strands in a cell?
49 Range part: Abbr.
50 Purge
51 Wasn't on commission
56 Cultural Revolution chief
59 Meter maid of song
60 Spy Aldrich
61 Wooer of Olive Oyl
63 Notes in a pot, maybe

64 Hop, skip or jump
65 Fabulous fellow?
66 Little swab
67 They may come with odds
68 Doesn't talk smoothly

DOWN

1 Splinter group
2 Goes off
3 The Phantom of the Opera's name
4 Day in Jerusalem
5 Kind of soup
6 Off track
7 Mutual fund fee
8 Announcer's medium
9 "I'm ready - let's hear it!"

10 Du ___ (menu phrase)
* 11 Enemy leader?
12 Actor Lugosi
13 Go sky-high
22 Bell-ringer of commercialdom
23 "That is so-o-o-o cute!"
26 Bagel variety
27 1930's director with three Oscars
28 Aunt Polly's creator
30 Bashar Assad's land
31 Shady spot
32 Single
33 Pilsener holder
34 Main line
36 Richie's mother, to Fonzie

40 Emphatic words of agreement
41 Mars, for one
43 Gallery event
44 C-worthy?
46 Singer Sumac
47 Understands
51 Old radio quiz show
52 Laugh ___
53 Small case
54 Ethnic acronym
55 Hindrance for Superman
56 Rumple
57 Perched on
58 Unwelcome word from a surgeon?
62 Rustic locale

by Philip Lew

ACROSS

1 "Air Music" composer
6 Town near Arches National Park
10 Answer the host
14 Final word
15 Solo, of a sort
16 Abbr. in a listing
17 Policy mates
19 Something to keep tabs on
20 Age abbr.
21 Dumas's Musketeers, e.g.
22 Was rude to
24 It may turn on a rooster
25 Belarus's capital
26 Olympic pool units
29 Argues an outcome
32 Orchard item
33 Hindu queen
34 Prevailed
35 Carol
36 With 29-Down, source of this puzzle's theme
37 Vocalist Vannelli
38 "___ bin ein Berliner"
39 Air traffic controllers stare at them
40 Asked
41 Southern taste treat
43 Drive-in employee
44 Big reptiles, informally
45 Big coca producer
46 Take over
48 Make reservations
49 General Motors division
52 Pout
53 Daily pastime for millions
* 56 Concert equipment
57 Thailand neighbor
58 Diarist Nin
59 Condé ___ (publisher)
60 Brontë woman
61 Gabber

DOWN

1 Risqué
2 Emanation
3 Reformer Jacob
4 Poetic contraction
5 Kind of gas
6 Donny's TV partner
7 Three-layer snack
8 Space
9 Baby's bed
10 Trash
11 Keeps
12 Farewell, to Cicero
13 Argued
18 Garden decorations
23 Chip in
24 Obscure
25 Early recordings
26 Excessively enthusiastic
27 Age
28 What drinking may cure
29 See 36-Across
30 Loyal sidekick
31 Pry
33 Spring events
36 First set of wheels, maybe
37 Swami
39 Mush
40 Treelined thoroughfare
42 Most loyal
43 Corp. bigwigs
45 Group on horseback, maybe
46 Mideast's Gulf of ___
* 47 A person in it is out of it
48 Rude person
49 1970's Plymouth ___ Fury
50 Rephrase
51 Bones, anatomically
54 Bit of hope?
55 Long-distance call starter

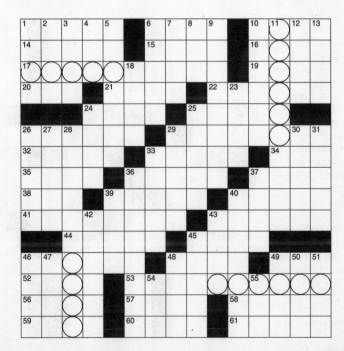

by William I. Johnston

ACROSS

1 Chew (on)
5 Busch Gardens locale
10 Italian wine region
14 First female U.S. Attorney General
15 Provide (with)
16 Descriptive dog name
17 On ___ (proceeding independently)
18 Makeshift punishment tool
19 Utters
20 You can't withdraw from them
23 Singer Tucker
24 Cluckers
25 Indian from whom a state name is derived
27 Weaselly
28 W.W. II fliers
31 Anchor man?
33 Receiver of blood samples
36 Actress Theda
37 Wide-awake and ready to go
41 Advertising catchword
42 Hurts like heck
43 Persian Gulf capital
46 "That's show ___!"
47 Many girls' middle names
* 50 Dallas-to-Houston dir.
51 House votes
54 In ___ (not yet born)
56 Sitcom feature
60 Corrida animal
61 Campus V.I.P.'s
62 Manhattan, e.g.
63 It's kept close to the chest
64 Touches ground
65 Costner role
66 Cruising
67 "Enigma Variations" composer
68 Editor's mark

DOWN

1 Transplants
2 Kind of network
3 "I come to bury Caesar, not to praise him" speaker
4 Lightheaded
5 Relative of a gull
6 Pastel hue
7 Ground cover
8 Factor
9 Stringed items
10 Part of N.A.A.C.P.: Abbr.
11 Pancake flippers
12 Hit film that included Mr. Potato Head
13 With 52-Down, words of agreement
21 Takes in
22 Olympic stadium cry
26 Failed 70's-80's polit. cause
29 "What a relief!"
30 Like a pancake
32 Egyptian art figure
33 Indian prey
34 Tray filler
35 Cutting remark
37 Some works by Michelangelo
38 Run through
39 "___ have any say in the matter?"
40 Feminist Bella
41 Frontier locales: Abbr.
44 Author Rand
45 Razz
47 High-flying clique
48 Words intended to scare
49 Most achy
52 See 13-Down
53 Like "hot-diggity"
55 Wheat crackers
57 ___ bene
* 58 Forever-day connector
59 Cold war inits.
60 1930's pub. works program

by Elizabeth C. Gorski

ACROSS

1 Prefix with sailing
5 They're made of whole cloth
10 Holiday music?
14 Toward the windless side
15 ___ Island Sound
16 Blue Bonnet product
17 Drape holders
18 Company once called Allegheny
19 Players wear masks for this
20 Start of a silly question
23 Treeless tract
24 Just enough to wet the lips
25 Frowning
28 Coat with plaster, say
31 Witch's laugh
33 Question, part 2
38 Rose's husband, on Broadway
39 Nonpareil
40 Study, and then some
41 Question, part 3
46 "Whoa, ___!"
47 Cozy
48 Draft letters
49 "Yay!"
51 CNN's Rowland
56 End of the question
59 1986 World Series site
62 Indian head, once?
63 Indian head, once
64 Chicken ___
65 Pontificate
66 Clearasil target
67 Emerald
68 59-Across player, in brief
69 Devour, in a way

DOWN

1 Home of L'Express
* 2 Overhead
3 Cover the gray again
4 "The Boy Who Cried Wolf" writer
5 "Doonesbury" cartoonist
6 "I understand," facetiously
7 Help during hard times
8 Shortens a sentence, maybe
9 1973 Pacino blockbuster
10 Funny Bishop
11 Chalet site, perhaps
12 End of a series

13 Pulitzer winner Akins
21 French twist, e.g.
22 On ___ with
25 Mini, midi or maxi
26 1942 Preakness winner
27 "The Silence of the Lambs" director
29 Yen
30 They may be tossed back
* 32 Multiple of XXXV
33 Bambi et al.
34 Awards since 1956
35 Small brooks
36 Vociferate
37 Marvel superheroes
42 Poop out

43 Loads, as a plate
44 That the sun will rise in the East, e.g.
45 Terse pans
50 Antediluvian
52 Half of the Odd Couple
53 Dorothy, to Em
54 Fashion's Karan
55 Put a stake in a pool
56 ★★★★ review
57 Ersatz
58 Yahoo.com, e.g.
59 Hit the slopes
60 ___ Holiness the Pope
61 It can be shocking

by Kelly Clark

ACROSS

1 Rice, e.g.: Abbr.
5 Category under "race," maybe
10 "That's gross!"
13 Book with legends
15 Russell of "Gladiator"
16 Second Amendment rights grp.
17 With 36- and 57-Across, an old dramatist's motto?
19 It's measured in MB
20 Pupils' surroundings
21 Buzzing with excitement
23 Light into
26 Like some sandwich bags
* 28 Work of 1606
30 Urgent request
31 Ph.D. hurdles
32 Northeastern Indians
35 Word after going or flat
36 See 17-Across
37 Cold, to Conchita
41 Truffles et al.
42 Creature under a bridge
43 Mr. Munster, of 60's TV
47 Work of 1604
49 Did
52 End of a blackmail letter
53 Sherpa's home
54 Brinks
56 Nutrition inits.
57 See 17-Across
62 Jr. and sr.
63 Goofed
64 Photographer Arbus
65 Port vessel
66 Roll-tops
67 Historic caravel

DOWN

1 Detroit org.
2 Mathematician's number
* 3 Elba, e.g., to Napoléon
4 Like some manufacturing costs
5 Publisher Adolph
6 Feller's targets
7 Simple basketball game
8 Farm female
9 Some Realtors' deals
10 Get ready to shower
11 Objects of quests
12 Work of 1604
14 One thing after another
18 Fight like a knight
22 Dickens cry
23 Boy with a bow
24 F.D.R.'s mother
25 Improvise, in a way
27 Brother of Seth
29 Axed
33 Tractor-trailer
34 Of the hipbone: Prefix
36 Polly, to Tom
37 "Wheel of Fortune" bonus
38 Craps play
39 Social problems
40 Facial tissue additive
41 Didn't serve well
42 Screw feature
43 Work of 1599
44 Curved bench
45 Meal
46 Elton John's longtime label
48 Duds
50 Tinker's target
51 The "10" in "10"
55 Cold war foe
58 Maximilian's realm: Abbr.
59 "Love Story" composer Francis
60 Writer Beattie
61 "___, verily"

by David Levinson Wilk

ACROSS

1 Where Sherlock Holmes "died," with "the"
5 Deejays' platters
10 Omnibus alternative
14 Ticked off
15 Ripley's last words?
16 Shakespearean ensign
17 Energy source
18 Get stuck
19 River of Aragón
20 Outsized sleeping accommodations?
23 Calypso offshoot
25 Long intro?
26 Blubbers
27 Too-small topper?
32 Where the action is
33 Thought: Prefix
34 Encircle
35 Like cheddar cheese on a tray
37 One of the Ivies
41 "Duck soup!"
42 H.M.O. requirement, usually
43 Too little of a bad thing?
47 Russian pancakes
49 Dawn goddess
50 Tale teller
51 Somewhat belated desire?
56 Ruination
57 Fess up
58 Pro ___
61 Dilly
62 Sailor's respite
63 Prolific auth.?
64 Noggin
65 Maze word
66 Seeds often get them

DOWN

* 1 Center of a comparison
2 His wife was a pillar
3 Vulgar sort
4 It might jackknife
5 Maturity classification of sherry
6 Move forward
7 ___-Aryan
8 Year-end libations
9 "Keep as is"
10 ___ del Fuego
11 Animal in a warren
12 Match, grammatically
13 They sometimes swing
21 Star in Lyra
22 Go off the wall?
23 Hose problem
24 Opera's ___ Te Kanawa
28 "Bitter" part
29 Nation with a solid green flag
30 Poetic homage
31 Nancy Drew's boyfriend
35 No-goodnik
36 Manipulate
37 Shortstop, e.g.: Abbr.
38 Spiritual revelation
39 Prefix with second
40 AMEX counterpart
41 Lighted sign
42 Dermatologist's diagnosis
43 Official seal
44 "Psst!" follower, maybe
45 Reason out
46 Hang out
47 Jazz variation
48 Thick vine
52 Brown rival
53 Where it all started
54 Latin 101 verb
55 Horseshoe ___
59 Last X of X-X-X
* 60 "T" or "F": Abbr.

by William A. Ballard

ACROSS

1 Snatches
5 Nuclear treaty result
8 Farm cry
14 Three-layer treat
15 Sport ___
16 Like a white rat
17 Cousin of a canvasback
18 E-mail address ending
19 Golf pro's concern
20 Spy movie catch phrase
23 It may be sold in yards
24 Crunches tighten them
25 Coffee holder
26 Tabloid photo subject
29 Cool cat
31 LP contents?
32 Ill humor
33 Calls up
35 More smart-alecky
36 Sampler sentiment
39 "Platoon" actor Willem
40 In addition
41 Pound sounds
42 "ER" extras
43 Slip away
47 "May I help you?"
48 "___ who?"
49 The fin man?
50 Morgan of the comics
* 51 1984 Cyndi Lauper #1 hit
55 Gives a clarion call
57 Pastoral place
58 Skip
59 Ply with food and drink
60 S.O.S part, supposedly
61 Parcel
62 Scully and Mulder, for two
63 Letter abbr.
64 Rabbit's title

DOWN

1 "I'm impressed!"
2 Pupil surrounder
3 Conked
4 Unloaded, in a way
5 Persistent problems
6 Quarks' places
7 Actress Campbell
8 Monopoly maker
9 John of song
10 Meir contemporary
11 Untouchable's belief
12 Mandela's org.
13 Misfortune
21 Freshmen's and sophomores' team
22 Clichéd movie ending
27 Turn tail
28 Anthem contraction
30 Self-produced CD's, maybe
31 Satisfies
32 Regional flora and fauna
34 Holiday since 1966
35 Ahab, e.g.
36 Also-ran of fable
37 Behind the scenes
38 Soldier Field crew
39 Kind of trader
42 Candy name
44 First coat
45 Arab, e.g.
46 Seat of Devonshire
48 Refine, as ore
49 Really enjoyed
52 Qom home
* 53 Angel's worry
54 Mummy's home
55 Undergarment
56 Drumstick

by Brendan Emmett Quigley

ACROSS

1 Big bash
5 Kind of printer
10 Hoops nickname
14 "Suuure!"
* 15 A lot up front?
16 Waiter's offering
17 Place with a famous address
19 Detail handler, maybe
20 Remote
21 Hockey great Howe
23 Further
24 Like many a high school sophomore
25 Underdog's goal
28 Soup ingredient
29 Balderdash
30 Kind of price
33 Weakens, as support
36 Reason for an "R" rating
38 Great Lakes fish
39 Antivenins
40 Gusto
41 Go to
43 Dangerous stretch of water
44 Clown props
46 Union issue
48 Best way to drive
50 Competitions
52 "Now!"
53 Skirt
57 Lummox
58 Penguins' home
60 Memo starter
61 Remove from memory
62 Pike
63 Clothes
64 Hannah of "Splash"
65 Some receivers

DOWN

1 Best Picture of 1958
2 Fortas and Vigoda
3 Mother of Apollo
4 Predecessor and successor of Churchill
5 Covets, with "after"
6 "Seascape" playwright
7 Kind of bolt
8 Get it wrong
9 Criticizing, slangily
10 Wisenheimers
11 German university town
12 Actress MacDowell
* 13 It can move in any direction
18 Noted conference center
22 Commonly, once
24 Property marker
25 Press
26 Bit of office fun
27 Council of Europe site
28 "Things to do" and others
31 Like some potatoes
32 Result of a 26-Down
34 Cheese region
35 Weakens
37 Diplomatic arrangements
42 Uncool sort
45 N.Y.C. subway
47 Guarantee
48 Bowling challenge
49 Town NE of Bangor
50 Itsy-___
51 The "Ishtar" of cars
53 Hollywood sighting
54 80's sci-flick
55 "Holy moly!"
56 Thesis penners
59 Belfast inits.

by Matt Gaffney

ACROSS

1 Price of a movie?
5 Wooer
9 Some figures on the Parthenon
14 Jacob's twin
15 Leave the stage
16 Become harvestable
17 Begin to wake up
18 Duchamp's art movement
19 Easy ___
20 British conservative's doctrine
22 Athenian or Corinthian
24 Place for a bar
26 "Carmen" and "Norma"
27 Bannockburn boy
28 Laverne and Shirley's landlady
30 Roster
33 Beige
35 Santa Anita doings
40 Composer Schubert
42 Yahoo! competitor
43 Miracle Whip maker
44 Al ___ (cooked yet firm)
45 Delta deposit
47 Nervous
48 Org. in which Colin Powell once served
50 Today, in Tijuana
52 Met villains, often
56 Tight-fisted folk
61 Oval
63 Drive back
64 Forest clearing
65 Inkling
67 Lavish affection (on)
68 Gourmand
69 Saxophone part
70 At any point
71 What foxhounds try to catch
72 Wraps up
73 Football linemen

DOWN

1 What two-piece suits lack
2 Retort in a playground argument
3 Nigerian currency
4 Agave
5 Nightstand spot
6 Closing period in a semester
7 Abet
8 Six-sided state
9 Part of Manhattan
10 Passenger train feature
11 Passenger train feature, maybe
* 12 Isabella, por ejemplo
13 Olden daggers
21 Girl "sweet as apple cider"
23 Long stretch
25 Herculean efforts
29 Lackluster
30 Mail abbr.
31 Load from a lode
32 Paddle
34 Playbill list
36 "Is it O.K. if I come in?"
37 One who may be slapped
* 38 Alphabet trio
39 Pigs' digs
41 Absolutely nothing
46 Clothes, slangily
49 C.I.A. predecessor
51 Alley ___
52 Sire
53 Object of many prayers
54 Old school item
55 Allies (with)
57 Belief system
58 Item kept on hand
59 Word with poly-
60 Prognosticators
62 Land west of Wales
66 Quiet sanctuary

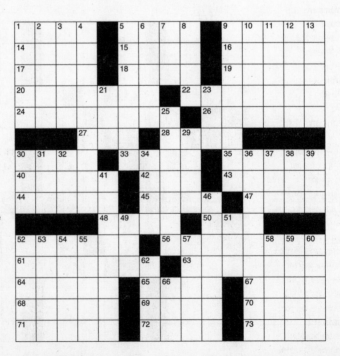

by Jim Morton

ACROSS

1 The oldest Brady kid
5 Scratches
10 Sleuths, for short
14 Like a certain avis
15 Museum item
16 1952 Winter Olympics site
* 17 First of billions
18 Trump
19 Knock for a loop
20 Mayfair moms
22 "The earth orbits the sun" and others, once
24 With 37- and 49-Across, possible solution to 12-Down
26 Brain popper
27 Disclose
30 Strumpet
33 Nazi fighter in W.W. II
36 As well
37 See 24-Across
41 U.S.S. Enterprise officer: Abbr.
42 Lab site: Abbr.
43 Old Studebakers
44 Furry-eared animals
47 Frost
49 See 24-Across
55 Symbol of Americanism
57 Astronomer's sighting
58 Like some points
59 Humble
61 It was sacred in ancient Egypt
62 Lothario's look
63 Decisive refusal
64 Salon job
65 Gung-ho (on)
66 Eyelid maladies
67 Ranch brush

DOWN

1 Pa's pa
2 Range of perception, so to speak
3 Goddess often pictured with a crown of roses
4 Angler's delight
5 Stick with a pocket
6 Romanian currency
7 Notwithstanding that, for short
8 Dentist's request
9 Ill-fated U.S. submarine of 1968
10 Difficult-to-predict outcome
11 Insurance worker
12 See 24-Across
13 Chips off the old block
21 Go back to brunette, say
23 Bark beetle's target
25 Paul Claudel play "The __ Slipper"
28 Hornswoggle
29 Gobblers
30 Bumpkin
31 Reverse
32 Predictor of things to come?
34 Electees
35 A tenth part
38 Kitchen basins
39 Look daggers
40 Servings on toast
45 Made carousel music
46 Had a heart?
48 One side in N.F.L. negotiations
50 Lhasa's land
51 Backbreaking
52 Northeast Sudan, once
53 Adhere
* 54 Waste maker
* 55 Book after Joel
56 Okefenokee resident
60 "What'd I tell ya?"

by Edgar R. Fontaine

ACROSS
1 Sudden start
5 Arrival of clouds, for instance
9 Use as a dining table
14 Read ___ (study)
15 Catamount
16 Towel material
17 Wampanoag war leader, 1675–76
19 "Oho!" and such
20 From the 1930's
21 Creek war leader, 1813–14
23 Mast support
25 First National Leaguer to hit 500 home runs
26 Matter of proof?
30 Seminole war leader, 1835–37
34 Electronic gate
35 Peak in Haute-Savoie
37 Opposing
38 Lenape advocate of Indian unity and resistance, ca. 1760's
42 ___-Aztecan languages
43 Laguna Veneta borderer
44 Temperature taker, maybe
45 Ottawa war leader, 1763–65
48 Gloom
50 Commanded
51 Bird so-called from its call
52 Shawnee war leader, 1812–13
56 TV ad directive
61 Like some colonies
62 Sauk war leader, 1832
64 Tutor's subject, maybe
65 Italian artist Guido
66 End ___
67 "Ivanhoe" writer
68 Mediterranean port
69 Huff

DOWN
1 Cause for an apology
2 Mimic
3 Any letter from A to G
4 Nibble
5 City north of Lisbon
6 Tight-lipped
7 Filer
8 Basketball's Thurmond
9 "And blah blah blah"
10 Freshen
11 H.S. class
12 City on the Oka
13 Wall Street Journal subj.
18 Tropical nut
22 Medicine man?
24 King who sacked Rome
26 Make sense
27 Deceive
28 List preceder
29 Harem room
30 Resist
31 Orangeish
32 Windblown soil
33 Pennies, maybe
36 Commanded
* 39 King and others
40 Next
41 Smile producer
46 Absentee
47 "You are, too!" preceder
49 Extra Strength product
51 Panther, e.g.
52 Shoe appendages
53 Like some struggles
54 "I'm history!"
55 Catalan river
57 Tough
58 Its work is done in stages
* 59 Can't pay
60 1970's–80's sitcom setting
63 Santa ___

by Robert B. Baker

ACROSS

1 Tree with a gourdlike fruit
7 Nail site
10 Hangup
13 Lackadaisical response
14 Hungarian patriot Nagy
16 Suffix with glass
17 Hits newsprint?
19 Bugs
20 "Primary Colors" author
21 "De amicitia" writer
23 Bring down
26 Paste
28 "Sicut ___ in principio" (church lyric)
29 Blubber
30 Talks gangster-style
★31 Rx amts.
★32 Add as a bonus
35 Decree of a sovereign
37 Like many Rod Serling works
38 More like Rod Serling works
41 Spanish babies, informally
43 In reality
44 Emulate Rembrandt, e.g.
46 C-D-G, e.g.
48 "Krazy" one
49 Emphatic aprobación
50 Jealous wife of myth
51 Rolls
53 Parlor item
55 Hotfoot it
57 Air tester: Abbr.
58 Items holding up teacher notices?
63 Naught
64 Defraud, slangily

65 "It's about time!"
66 Memphis-to-Nashville dir.
67 1960's march organizer: Abbr.
68 Go out of business

DOWN

1 325i maker
2 Sound at a spa
3 Put ___ show
4 Subsidizes
5 Achilles reflex site
6 Pedestal
7 Bench sites
8 One coulomb/second
9 Ruins an oboe?
10 Flotsam on the Mississippi?
11 Open

12 Stupefies
15 "___ tu" (song sung by Renato)
18 Galileo, notably
22 Et ___
23 Wine region
24 ___ theory, in physics
25 Rodeo yarn?
27 Book checker, for short
30 Grain inspections?
33 Kind of wonder
34 Carry the day
36 Foul caller
39 "L'___, c'est moi"
40 Turns
42 1887 romance novel
43 Athenian lawgiver

44 Sect member around the time of Christ
45 Haberdashery item
47 Bean and others
★51 People are picky about this
52 "Darn ___!"
54 Bend in a river
56 King in an Elgar work
59 Eclipsed
60 Low one
61 Wildcats of the Big 12 Conf.
62 Big Nascar advertiser

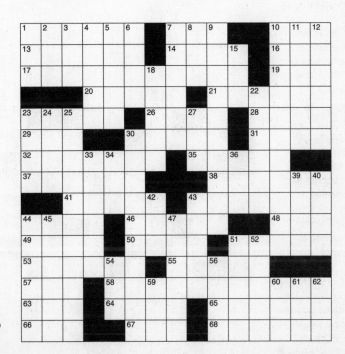

by Robert H. Wolfe

ACROSS

1 Golden gifts from Gaea
7 Dematerializes
15 Any Australian girl
16 So pretty
17 Blasé remark after a defeat
19 Extensively
20 ___ canto
21 Richmond-to-Norfolk dir.
22 Shutout team's score
23 Automaton
25 Blab
29 Prepare for a snap
31 Doorpost
34 Teachers' advocate: Abbr.
35 "Game" played to get information
39 Bug out
41 Camp facility
42 1991 comedy of the sexes
* 44 Word with red or army
45 Pigeon coop
46 Impersonated
48 "Hey, I never thought of that!"
50 Refuse to recognize
53 Ho Chi Minh Trail locale
55 Eyeball
58 Kicker?
59 It's active in Sicily
60 Sporadic
65 Drawer odorizer
66 Some scouts
67 Knickknacks
68 Git into a rough-and-tumble

DOWN

1 Temple of Isis site
2 Alexander the Great's father
3 Ones looking at sentences
4 Letter-to-Santa enclosure
5 "Rockaria!" rock group
6 "Little" children's book character
7 San Pablo Bay city
8 Misspent energy
9 Roman ___
10 Furies
11 MS. accompaniers
* 12 "The Chris Rock Show" shower
13 Wood with a twisted, spiral grain
14 Find out
18 It twists and turns
23 Lined with crystals
24 Sweet sap source
26 Phone calls, room service charges, etc.
27 No. 10 in a list
28 Goggle
30 Highball ingredient
32 Degs. for execs
33 Historic 1942 surrender site
36 Numbskull
37 Charges
38 Sink sound
39 Hairstyle
40 Casino game
43 Rides
47 1973 Elton John hit
49 Navajo home
51 Pained comment?
52 Allude
54 Parson's home
56 What stripes may indicate
57 Dwell
59 Dairy aisle section
60 Cast one's vote
61 Post Office motto word
62 Friend abroad
63 Court bisector
64 Trip planner: Abbr.

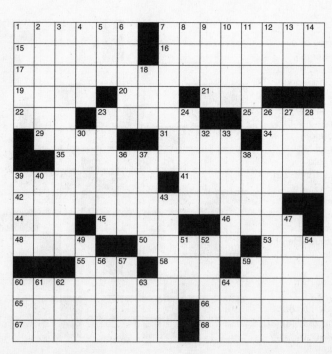

by Patrick Berry

ACROSS

1 "I Spy" co-star
5 Opening device
8 "Lycidas" poet
14 Kind of account
15 From ___ Z
16 Melodic
17 Wuss
19 Change the agenda
* 20 Clear-cut
22 Above reproach
23 De Valera's land
24 Raised
26 Improvised, in a way
29 Standard advice for a bride
33 Square dance group
34 Kicks
35 Brooks or Allen
36 Average, e.g.
37 N.F.L. Hall-of-Famer George
38 Austin of "Knots Landing"
* 39 One in the service?
40 Solved
41 Long for
42 Cottonwood relatives
44 "Macbeth" figures
45 Indelicate
46 Warm-up
47 1949 Cagney film
50 Many a yard sale item
55 Forgives, as an offense
57 Advance
58 Popped up
59 Have
60 Erupter of 1992
61 Dangerous job
62 Fed. hush-hush group
63 Settle

DOWN

1 Scour
2 Orenburg's river
3 Priest of the East
4 Diner souvenir
5 Sleeveless tunic worn over a knight's armor
6 Expiate
7 Singer Bill known as the Cowboy Rambler
8 Impair
9 Not at all resentful
10 Fat stuff
11 Kind of call
12 Anthem opening
13 Asian, e.g.
18 Did half a biathlon
21 Conventional
25 Officiates
26 "Ballad of John Henry" folk singer
27 Malfunction
28 Highest peak in the Philippines
29 Orders to go?
30 "In other words . . ."
31 Brass
32 They usually do no harm
34 Singer who formed the Love Unlimited Orchestra
37 Old antisubversive group
38 Den decorations
40 Din
41 Barely moved
43 Buildup
44 "The Real McCoys" co-star of 50's–60's TV
46 Team followers
47 Lab subject
48 "My ___!"
49 Dubai V.I.P.
51 Study of G.D.P. and such
52 Not supporting
53 "Cats" director Trevor
54 Durable wood
56 ___-cone

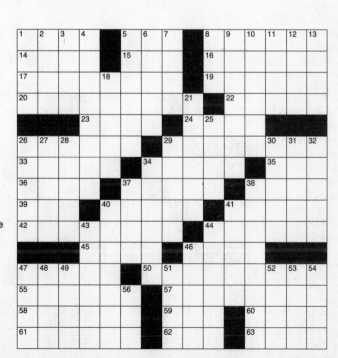

by Rich Norris

ACROSS

1 Old Jewish scholars
6 Accelerator suffix
10 Like some museumgoers
14 Low place
15 Kosovo combatant
16 Knock around
17 Travels with Sinbad, in a way
20 Certain colonist
21 Shadow
22 It may precede "mañana"
23 Knead-y one?
25 Become disenchanted
27 The Beatles and the Dave Clark Five, in a way
32 Like a slug
35 Place for portraits
36 8 pts.
37 Sign to read
38 Chopping firewood, e.g.
40 ___ breve
* 41 Like Bruckner's Symphony No. 7
42 Increase sharply
43 Super Bowl sight
44 Identical, in a way
48 Bore
49 Duchamp's mustachioed Mona Lisa, e.g.
53 Inverted "e"
56 Statistics calculation
57 Glaswegian's refusal
58 Gold, frankincense and myrrh, in a way
62 Pull down
63 Fighting
64 ___ the hole

65 St. Paul's architect
66 Tree growth
67 Yes or no follower

DOWN

1 Black tea source
2 Safari boss
3 Prepares to cast
* 4 Word before and after "in"
5 Sonnet parts
6 Vacation memento, maybe
7 Tape recorder part
8 Tolkien beast
9 "ER" network
10 Winner of two Triple Crowns
11 Mythical fliers
12 Mediator's skill
13 Disco standard
18 Lacking play
19 Boorish sort
24 Leave slack-jawed
25 Old phone's lack
26 Look like a wolf
28 Cause of side discomfort?
29 Wrinkly fruit
30 Pilot's place?
31 Prelude to a duel
32 Be het up
33 Hawks' former home
34 Carnival weirdo
38 Nightclub of song
39 Reagan Cabinet member
40 "A New Life" director

42 Floral display
43 Barrio businesses
45 The Perfect Fool
46 Mythical dreamboat
47 Stationery store purchases
50 Conclude
51 "Mercure" composer
52 Intervening, in law
53 Lather
54 Blacken
55 Epitaph starter
56 Miracle workers of '69
59 Verb for Popeye
60 Telephone trio
61 French 55-Down

by Bonnie S. Prystowsky

ACROSS

1 Rebounds, e.g.
5 Pioneer automaker
9 Ill-prepared
14 Word with Red or ant
15 Galba's predecessor
16 "Lorenzo's Oil" star, 1992
17 Chicken (out)
18 Clever accomplishment
19 Bakery goodie
20 Proceeds boldly
23 "Potent Potables for 200, __"
24 __ piece (consistent)
25 Adventurer played by Douglas Fairbanks Jr.
28 Approached
33 It's grounded
34 Golfer's accessory
36 Muse of history
37 Doesn't go in single file
41 Give the look to
42 To whom a fakir prays
43 Mom's specialty, for short
44 Some plastic surgery
47 Seychelles money
49 Part of a price
50 Top
51 Shows shock
58 "Golden Boy" playwrite
59 Jerusalem's Mosque of __
60 Result of a dam, perhaps
62 Go together
63 Drop
64 Word to a C.B. operator
65 Bait
66 "It Was a Lover and His __" (old song standard)
67 Damp

DOWN

1 Prop for a magician's trick
2 Kind of function
3 It's found in a round
4 Rare blood designation
5 One way to buy things
6 Pope who created the Schism of 1054
7 Regulated item
8 Certain student, for short
9 Wobbly, say
10 "Impossible"
11 __-eyed
12 Peak in Catania province
* 13 Put down one's ball
21 Poles, e.g.
22 Name repeated in a nursery rhyme
25 Attach, as a patch
26 Adult insect
27 Cancels
28 Relaxes, with "down"
29 Asia's __ Sea
30 Send
31 Window alternative
32 Univ. military programs
35 Clear the deck?
38 Maintain the pace
39 Mixed drink servers
40 Any point on a mariner's compass
45 Hardly stay-at-homes
46 __ pro nobis
* 48 It may be shelled
* 50 First name in diaries
51 Kind of cheese
52 Leg up
53 __ limit
54 Brown & Williamson brand
55 Flaubert heroine
56 Sheltered spot
57 Understood
61 Like some wines

by Joe DiPietro

ACROSS

1 Best-selling female writer of 1922
10 Temper
*15 Place for hand-holding?
16 Fifty minutes past
17 Bridge dream
18 Ninnies
19 Arm of the U.N., e.g.
20 Red sushi fish
21 Magician's hiding place
22 New deal
24 Baseball dream
26 Missile's trajectory
28 Agreement
29 Golf dream
34 Fuzz
38 Ticket category
39 Compose
40 New York Life competitor
41 Soccer star Mia
42 Gridiron dream
44 Star turns
47 One of the Ewings, on "Dallas"
48 Hockey dream
52 Crone
57 Eastern hospice
58 Exclamation of impatience
60 Capitol feature
61 Dot on a computer screen
62 Pinochle dream
64 Uses
65 "Man, that's fun!"
66 Spanish direction
67 Big Sunday dinners, maybe

DOWN

1 Actress Samantha
2 "The Simpsons" character
3 Popular computers
4 Austrian-born Tony winner, 1955
5 Stock page abbr.
6 Part just above a horse's hoof
7 Syllables before "Di" and "Da" in a Beatles song
8 Assassinated
9 Pro ___
10 Leaning to the right?
11 Moved
12 Where many an island is found
13 Computer pioneer Wozniak
14 Car wash employee
21 ___ Na Na
23 Café additive
25 Police order
27 Liturgical language
*29 "So there!"
30 Harem room
31 ___ and Abner, old comedy duo
32 Horror film locale
33 Modern
35 "Am ___ blame?"
36 Cap'n's heading
37 Whip but good
40 "Alas!"
43 Feature of many a hotel event
45 "You'll regret it otherwise!"
46 Soused
48 A big body in Africa
49 ___ a minute
50 Street fleet
51 Japan's capital until 1868
53 Writer ___ Rogers St. Johns
54 They're popular in Israeli circles
55 "___ to Avoid" (1966 hit)
56 Sign on a saloon door
59 Locale of Vict. and N.S.W.
62 Party preparation
63 Wall St. action

by Bob Sefick

ACROSS

1 Nears, with "on"
9 Animal shelter
13 Paper-folding creation
14 Like a rainbow
16 Huey
19 Dancing Astaire
20 "Now I remember!"
21 Fertility clinic stock
22 "___ do"
23 Enjoy a rose
24 Skelton's Kadiddlehopper
* 25 Scale tone
26 Tucks away
27 Tippler
28 Frau's abode
29 Land of Robert Burns
30 Dewey
35 Humorous illustrator ___ Searle
36 Not be calm
37 Oscar-nominated role of 1966
38 King's word
39 Econ. figure
42 Latch (onto)
43 It may be waxed
44 Memories of a whirlwind trip, maybe
45 38-Down's home: Abbr.
46 Pipe cleaner
47 Like sod
48 Louie
51 Full of chutzpah
52 Stets
53 Roasting platform
54 1968 pitcher with six consecutive shutouts

DOWN

1 Orient Express terminus, once
2 Misled
3 "Big Brother is watching you" writer
4 Ecodisaster
5 Besides
6 Pedro or Paulo
7 Well-known, but not well-liked
8 Huey, Dewey and Louie
9 Mike holder
10 Makeshift cradle
11 Hosp. ward
12 Unwavering
15 Gets down to work
17 Brother Castor and sister Olive
18 Attacked
23 Mike holder
24 Kind of skin
26 Rock that may hold fossils
27 Longtime "Today" show personality
29 Contractor's info
* 30 Like "Othello"
31 Continues, after a fashion
32 Nebulous
33 Critically injure
34 Jean Valjean, at the start of "Les Misérables"
38 Overseas carrier
39 Tongue, anatomically
40 Cooking agent
41 "The Scarlet Letter" woman
43 Doesn't wear well
44 ___ stiff
46 7th-century date
47 Relig. leaders
49 Tax form info: Abbr.
50 Kind of care

by Mark Diehl

ACROSS

1 They may be out on a limb
6 After the hour
10 Have no truck with
14 On the ball
15 Capital captured by the Germans on 4/9/40
16 Bishop of Rome
17 Sylvester's "Rocky" co-star
*18 Most close
*20 Plan B
22 "When you get ___ . . ." (parent's reply)
23 Russian retreat
27 Formed fuzzballs
30 Kind of needle
32 In the thick of
33 Denizen of the deep
35 Place for bacon
36 Airplane maneuverer
38 Guitarist Paul
39 A toddler may go on one
41 Lincoln picture site
42 Get ready for a comeback tour
43 Doesn't hold back
45 Captain Hull, known as "Old Ironsides"
46 Maintenance mate
48 Football play
54 Act of betrayal
57 Gen. Powell
58 Enchanted prince, perhaps
59 Skip
60 Electronic game pioneer
61 Where to wear a genouillère

62 Gets the picture
63 Conviction

DOWN

1 Abbr. in many org. names
2 Carrier to 54-Down
3 Actress Ward
4 Having three parts
5 Clip alternative
6 Follower of tracks, maybe
7 Moving
8 Stitch target
9 Novelist Morrison
10 Soufflé flavorer
11 It makes a row
12 Bull markets
13 Like some prices
19 Founder

21 "How ___!"
24 Fireplace site
25 Moon of Saturn named after an Amazon
26 Bikini tryouts
27 Scrolls
28 Some computer files
29 Ancient Romans spoke it
30 Fix
31 Letter on some college jackets
33 Move after a pirouette, perhaps
34 Club ___
36 High points
37 N.Y.C. subway
40 Fit to be tied
41 Mean

43 Abbr. after a name
44 Sweet grape used in winemaking
46 Count with a keyboard
*47 Sacks, so to speak
49 Win category in the W.B.A.
50 Coleridge work
51 Flair
52 Frigid finish
53 Sweater
54 See 2-Down
55 Samovar
56 John ___

by Greg Staples

ACROSS

1 Unhurried
5 ___ Hashana
9 Works in the Uffizi Palace
*13 Fortress on a hill
*15 Regarding
16 Movie princess
17 Man in a suit
18 Creator of 35-Across
20 Approves, in a way
22 Quattro maker
23 Ice grp.
24 Not just one
25 Crew members
27 Jane ___
28 Like old postcards
30 Parents, often
32 Rodeo catcher
34 Velvet finish?
35 Popular fictional 31-Down
39 One with a match?
40 Retinue
41 Outdo in
44 Active volcanoes, e.g.
48 "Go on . . ."
49 Friday companion
52 Aware of
53 Maglie of 1950's baseball
54 New York-area college
55 Entrance
57 Favorite sport of 35-Across
60 Singer Crystal
61 Forearm bone
62 ___ Te Kanawa
63 Tanks and such
64 Times for les vacances
65 "Light" and "dark" orders
66 Homes in the hills

DOWN

1 Japanese port near Nagasaki
2 Pressure
3 Rococo
4 Subject taught at 35-Across's school
5 Rule of India
6 "Ship of Fools" actor Werner
7 Play, in a way
8 Like monks
9 Unstinting amount
10 Comet, for one
11 Small-time
12 Super Bowl XV team
14 Down
19 Lush
21 U-boat detector
26 "The Practice" role: Abbr.
29 Always, poetically
31 See 35-Across
33 Clever
35 It may get your attention
36 Roughly
37 Not live
38 Standoff
39 Competitor of 22-Across
41 Language with no known relative
42 Boric ___
43 Three-horse carriage
45 Catalyst of a sort
46 Container with a rotating ball
47 Doesn't look pleased
50 Sammy Kaye's "___ Tomorrow"
51 "___ bleu!"
*56 Eastern title
*58 Court figs.
59 Part of H.R.H.

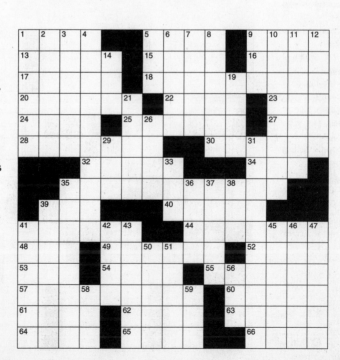

by David J. Kahn

ACROSS

1 Area sweeper?
6 Flexible, in a way
10 Isn't gentle with
*14 ___ Castle
15 Sour fruit
16 Substitution in a list
17 Condescend
18 Endorse
19 Tabula ___
20 Radicals' bash?
23 Muralist Rivera
25 O. Henry plot twists
26 Excellent hip-hop affair?
29 "What ___ to do?"
30 One who hits the high notes
31 Blender button
35 Calls after bad calls
37 Shipboard title: Abbr.
39 N.Y.C. cultural center
40 Nay sayers
42 Tennessee's state flower
45 1986 U.S.S.R. launch
46 Doctors' frolic?
50 Bolsters the confidence of
53 Best Supporting Actor of 1999
54 Physicists' fete?
57 Director Kazan
58 Pinkish
59 Riverbank romper
63 Kind of car
64 Part of G.M.T.
65 Afresh
66 Daly of "Judging Amy"
67 Rosie O'Donnell's Muppet friend
68 Wind

DOWN

1 Free (of)
2 Exist en masse
3 "Agnus ___"
4 One who's casting about?
5 Broke a promise
6 Like certain profs.
7 Second-century date
8 Goldbricks
9 Middling beginning?
10 How some interest is paid
11 Arcade pioneer
12 Not be frugal
13 Emulates St. George
*21 Convergence points
22 Lowdown
23 Friend of Pythias
24 Blithering sort
26 Cake with a kick
27 Time to look ahead
28 Pre-exam feeling, maybe
32 Like 7-Down
33 1960's middleweight champ Griffith
34 Title for Robert Walpole
36 Feign
38 ___ Lanka
41 Withered
43 Atahualpa subject
44 Peppers, perhaps
47 Peter Ustinov autobiography
48 Judean Plateau locale
49 Attacked by mosquitoes
50 "___ of robins in her hair"
51 Tarnish
52 Grafting shoot
55 Vampire chronicler Stoker
56 Major NBC star
60 Company once owned by Howard Hughes
61 Cousin of a moose
62 Part of a Reuben

by Gene Newman

ACROSS

1 "A miss ___ good . . ."
5 "Excuse me . . ."
9 Swindler, slangily
14 Hardly the pick of the litter
15 When said three times, a W.W. II movie
16 Prayer starter
17 Utah ski resort
18 Like many an I.R.A.
20 Octet's peculiarity?
22 Year in Justinian I's reign
23 Happy baby talk
27 "Et tu, Brute?," e.g.?
30 Scene of W.W. I fighting
32 Well-behaved
33 Writer-critic Hentoff
34 Biol. course
35 Cast
37 Eyeball
38 Night off for Scheherazade?
39 Norwegian hero
40 Cause fuzzy vision
41 One who babbles "baa, baa"?
* 45 On the move
* 46 "Perfectly clear, man!"
47 What pollution in the Sargasso Sea may lead to?
53 Do an autumn job
56 Imitation butter
57 Hokkaido port
58 ___ Diner
59 It may be polished

60 Like sudden-death playoffs
61 "Dragonwyck" author Seton
62 Gabs

DOWN

1 Modern site of ancient Nineveh
2 Officer in the original "Star Trek"
3 Not a pro
4 Hoagy Carmichael classic
5 For three: Fr.
6 Walk
7 ___ Stanley Gardner
8 Bamako is its capital
9 Divinity
10 Many
11 Election time: Abbr.
12 Before, once
13 N.Y.C.'s ___ Drive
19 Cold weather drink
21 "The Twittering Machine" artist
24 Destination of some pilgrims
25 City SSE of Gainesville
26 Web-footed swimmer
27 Like many an English inn
28 "Uncle!"
29 Suffix with ball
30 Bambino watcher

31 Granddaddy of all computers
35 Bamboozle
36 Barrister's concern
37 June 14 display
39 Useful
40 High-calorie cheese
42 Defunct Texas team
43 Uxorial
44 Where Leon Trotsky grew up
48 ___ Sutra
49 Cooker
50 Hip bones
51 Chain site
52 Operates
53 Become unusable
* 54 Took the cake?
55 Neb. neighbor

by Manny Nosowsky

ACROSS

1 Stupido
6 Per
10 Mountain ___
14 Big band?
15 California's ___ Valley
16 City on the Oka
17 Head, jocularly
18 They have whiplike tails
20 Truck stop
22 Forgo
23 "Moonlight" and "Farewell"
27 Very distant, as space
30 Prove wrong
31 Snow showers?
34 Bullets, to bettors
36 Mideast port
37 "C'est la vie"
40 Secret language
41 Orbital path, usually
42 2.4-mil. member union
43 Got back together
45 Silents star Jannings
47 Child of the cartoons
49 Put under
54 Nursery rhyme meal
57 Heading maintainer
60 Pick up
61 Word with black or fire
62 Queen abandoned by Aeneas
63 "Frasier" dog
64 Sort
65 "Voice of Israel" author
66 California's Point

DOWN

1 Very impressed
2 Speaker's 3 × 5 cards, e.g.
3 Caper
4 Ask for hay, say?
5 Deeply embedded
6 Like some coaches: Abbr.
7 Hummus holder, maybe
8 Leaves undone
9 Gear with a small number of teeth
10 Renewed
11 Portfolio part, for short
12 E or G, e.g.
13 Golfer Ernie
* 19 Passed

21 Exertion
24 Enough to wet one's lips
25 Some hotel lobbies
26 Limitless quantities
28 Repeat
29 Something to complain about
31 Confused, informally
32 Hard to pin down
33 No longer warm
35 Stroked
37 Swabbies
38 Promotion
39 Adjust
44 Mock
46 Soup kitchen worker

48 Impromptu
50 Person from Malmö
51 Like a con artist's business
52 Mysterious
53 Force units
55 Pop
56 Immensely
57 Perfect
* 58 News letters
59 Acquisition for some vacationers

by Joe DiPietro

ACROSS

1 One of the Reagans
6 One flu source
10 Italian artist Bernini
14 Spanish skating figures
15 Some ballpoints
16 Tense
17 Reprieve
20 Repeated phrase in a children's verse
21 Tibia connectors
22 Preschooler
23 Rancher's enemy
26 Bounding site?
28 Contemptible one
31 Heraldic hue
32 Ford product, briefly
33 Merry king
34 What higher prices may produce
37 Members of the flock
38 Code word
39 Plumped for
40 Court figs.
41 Late-60's fashion item
42 Depressing
43 Jesus, with "the"
44 Gang business's need
46 Part of a Washington address?
53 Hedonistic
54 Roar producer
55 "___ yellow ribbon . . ."
56 Prefix with magnetic
57 "___ Ben Adhem" (Leigh Hunt poem)
58 Handycam maker
59 Corners

DOWN

* 1 American Legion place
2 Pituitary gland output
3 Ethnic cuisine
4 Top spots?
5 Sets apart
6 Encourages
7 90 . . . or a good title for this puzzle?
8 Where the Althing sits: Abbr.
9 They make do without
10 "Do you understand?"
11 Answer to 10-Down
12 Wowed
13 Part of an Empire State Bldg. address
18 Can
19 Over
23 Looked over, in a way
24 Boston Symphony Orchestra leader
25 Wassailers' times
27 Domingo delivery
28 Moving line
29 Tagamet target
30 Like some pipes
32 Four kings, maybe
33 Steward
35 Replay causes
36 "Haw!"
41 Feature of a lunar landscape
42 Big name in fruit
43 Muddle
* 45 Speak again
* 46 "Itself," in a phrase
47 Triple-decker
48 Prefix with magnetic
49 Fiddlers for 33-Across, e.g.
50 Foreign money
51 Memo starter
52 I's

by Manny Nosowsky

58 OPEN SEASON

ACROSS

1 Plank's place, perhaps
11 Nevada's Sen. Harry ___
15 What a tippler might have
16 "___ Imroth" (Sandburg poem)
17 Think about changing
18 Scanty
19 "Jerry Maguire" director
20 Put on
21 They may be directed toward the back
22 Pack ___
23 First name in game shows
24 Cracker topper
25 Nada
26 Health store snack bar ingredient
27 OK, in a way
28 Fast follower
30 Certain crown material
32 Zoning board calculation
34 R.P.I. grad, perhaps
35 In the rear
37 It may be at your fingertips
41 Some games require them
42 PC support staff
45 Crackerjack
46 A film might receive one
47 Louise and others
48 Ready
49 On its way
50 Biology lab supply
51 Caffeinated concoction
52 European leader?
53 Some people work on it
55 Pet
* 56 "Some help would be nice, folks!"
57 Some vacationers' acquisitions
58 Emulates Scheherazade

DOWN

1 Like some pen residents
2 Lack of get-up-and-go
3 Shows alarm
4 Nevil Shute's "___ Like Alice"
5 Pitch
6 Selene's sister
7 Happy sort
8 Tried, with "at"
9 Spoiled
10 Lighted stacks
11 Show of disapproval
12 Blow up
* 13 OK, in a way
14 Producer of a distress call?
23 Done less?
26 Astronomical discovery of 1801
27 Olympic racers
29 Ore-Ida product
31 Egyptian symbols of life
33 Sophocles tragedy
35 Wave catcher
36 Double
38 Not full
39 Polish remover
40 "That ___ . . ."
41 Respond to 56-Across
43 Crown coverer
44 West Coast artists' colony site
47 Like some agreements
48 Muhammad Ali was one
51 Future atty.'s hurdle
54 Tags

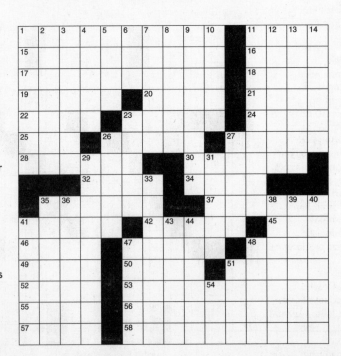

by Noah Dephoure

ACROSS

1 Locale receiving investments
16 Newspaper feature
17 Quick-sketch pros
* 18 Certain clamp shapes
19 Flirts may use theirs
20 Zairean autocrat Mobutu ___ Seko
21 Kind of test
22 Summer feature: Abbr.
24 Head
27 Codger
29 Addressee of many a request
32 Possible result of hesitation
36 Hobbies and such
37 Paris premiere of 1953
38 Patty Hearst kidnap grp.
39 Insouciance
40 Western Electric founder ___ Barton
41 Abbr. on mariners' maps
42 Guff
45 Computer picture
48 Spot
49 Bug-eyed
53 Ballpark figures
57 Memorable Met conductor
58 Gives cause for optimism

DOWN

1 Fam. tree member
2 1982 George Plimpton best-seller
3 ___ infra (see below)
4 Form of the verb "etre"
5 Fan setting
6 Declaim
7 Command
8 Acknowledge
9 Old musical notes
10 Big mfr. of point-of-sale terminals
11 Day care attendee
12 Most-wanted
13 Dodge
14 CPR pros
15 Handle: Fr.
21 Standard late-night TV fare
22 29-Across, often
23 Playwright Preston
24 Central
25 Port of ancient Rome
26 Bickering, say
28 "___ take arms against a sea of troubles": Shak.
29 Botch
30 Four Holy Roman emperors
31 Popular computer game
* 32 See 33-Down
* 33 With 32-Down, things that send people to jail
34 Gluttons
35 Brightly colored
41 Small bone of the middle ear
43 Strike ___
44 Lip-___ (fakes it)
45 Mark of Zorro?
46 "The Last of the Mohicans" girl
47 Con man?
48 ___ perpetuum (let it be everlasting)
49 Football Hall-of-Famer Marchetti
50 "What ___!" ("That's rich!")
51 Kind of therapy
52 "No returns"
54 Prior to, to Prior
55 Help wanted notice?
56 "I see!"

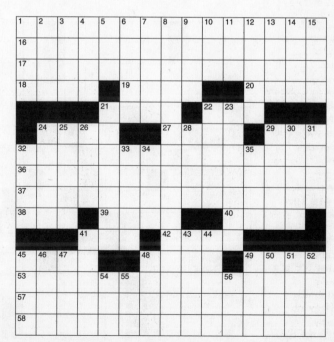

by Martin Ashwood-Smith

60 EQUAL PARTS

ACROSS
1 Golden item in a Rimsky-Korsakov title
4 It's a part of life
9 Bibliographical abbr.
14 With 47-Down, hot
15 Pacifists' protest
16 Dark times in Dijon
17 Like some genetic laws
19 Some are thrown for it
20 Became loaded
22 Gala's husband and portraitist
23 "Who Will Answer?" singer
27 Pro wrestling's "Raw __"
31 "I'm all ears!"
32 Fed. auditors
35 Cardinal's title
37 Duke of __ (Philip II's adviser)
39 Take care of a fly
40 Barely made it home?
41 Kind of engineer
44 Has too much, briefly
45 20 hundredweights
46 Ranger, e.g.
48 It bought Carnation in 1985
49 Charge
52 Theme of this puzzle
58 It gets many touchdowns
61 Capital
62 St. __ (children's hospital)
63 It's everything
64 Howard Hughes acquired it
65 Dawn
66 Like a dragon
67 Pilothouse abbr.

DOWN
1 Part of S.E.C.: Abbr.
2 Start of a millennium
3 Press conference activity
4 Like the artist Rubens
5 Actress Taylor
6 Concern of optométrie
7 100 dinars
8 Years in Hadrian's reign
9 Ad infinitum
10 Beats
11 Half of a 1955 merger
* 12 Name in 1995 news
13 Kitchen amt.
18 Links locale
21 Like a mama's boy?
24 College near Palo Alto
25 Castilian hero
26 Olympic racers
28 Dried up
29 "__ sure you know . . ."
30 Defeat again, in a way
32 French-speaking locale
33 Dress with a flare
34 Woodwind section
36 Often
38 When "To be or not to be" is recited
42 Least profane
43 One way to be bound
47 See 14-Across
50 Certifies
* 51 Some races
53 They're coming out
54 Firm head
55 March Madness org.
56 Living __
57 Warehouse
58 Concern of optometría
59 Barbarian
60 A lot of junk mail

by M. Francis Vuolo

ACROSS

1 Iron hook with a handle
* 5 Place to have locks changed
15 Bus or air alternative
16 Bach wrote a concerto in A for it
17 With 10-Down, "Charmaine" songwriter
18 Articulate
19 ___ roll
20 New York Cosmos star
21 Discharge
22 It's interested in interest
24 "The Oblong Box" writer
26 Spawn
27 "Which Way ___?" (1977 film)
29 File holder
33 Pirate of note
37 1980 Rolling Stones hit
38 Binds
39 Let the cat out of the bag
40 Crescent point
41 South extension
42 Flee
43 One of Hines's varieties
46 Like a 16-Across
50 Fan's production
52 Stretch, with "out"
53 Some animals are close to it
56 Bahrain power?
57 Part of a forest bed
58 Doing
59 Paloverde and pecan
60 "A Kind of Loving" novelist Barstow

DOWN

1 Nod to, maybe
2 Exasperation exclamation
3 You may dip into it at dinner
4 Impresario Ziegfeld
5 Not erect
6 Director Gance
7 Auditioner's quest
8 ___ and the Dragon (book of the Apocrypha)
9 Mad people, for short?
10 See 17-Across
11 Unpleasant hangover?
12 Jazz (up)
13 Bonanza finds
14 Cooped
20 Look through a keyhole
23 Malodorous: Var.
24 Exercise unit
25 35-Down, for one
27 Radioactive isotope having mass 230
28 Gets lost
29 It may be burning
30 Having ignored a subpoena, perhaps
31 Overpower
32 Couple in contact?
33 "La Vie Bohème" musical
34 1847 tale of the South Seas
35 Musical premiere of 1900
36 Part of a shower scene?
42 Novelist ___ Reid Banks
43 Points at dinner
44 Dog with a curled-back tail
45 1940's–50's dictator
46 Lifters count them
47 Turnoff
48 Burial place of the Greek giant Enceladus
* 49 Down less
50 Like some loads
51 Can you dig it?
54 This, to Héloïse
55 Rx word
56 Linz locale: Abbr.

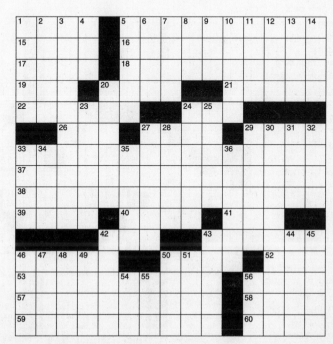

by Brendan Emmett Quigley

ACROSS

1 Tag sale tag
5 Arab patriarch
10 Crumpled
14 20-0 win, e.g.
15 Little wriggler
16 Lena of "Havana"
* 17 Good buddy
18 1950's sitcom star
19 Alliance
20 With 37-Across, what the music critic said about 55-Across?
22 Stag
23 Pillow material
24 Drench
26 Kind of service
27 Union ___: Abbr.
28 Nicholas of ___, patron saint of mariners and thieves
32 Drug
34 Electrify
36 Things that help people to carry on?
37 See 20-Across
40 Phlebitis targets
41 Salt
42 White Rabbit's cry
44 Opp. of legato, in music
45 Idled
48 Photo ___
49 High-tech program, for short
51 "A Tree Grows in Brooklyn" woman ___ Nolan
53 They may be odd
55 This puzzle's subject, born 7/21/1920
59 Press
60 "Semper Fidelis" composer
61 No. 2
62 Second starter
63 Not so new
64 Result of a gas shortage
65 Load
66 Young dragonfly
67 Support system?

DOWN

1 Curves
2 "Very well"
3 Mrs. Marcos
4 Shooting ___
5 Czech, e.g.
6 One with big ears
7 Marine birds
8 Six Russian czars and grand dukes
9 Instruments seldom seen in orchestras
10 Oodles
11 Ration out
12 Broken
13 55-Across has played many of these
21 Auto amenities
25 1970's fad
29 Pointer's cry
30 Hightails it
31 Dolts
33 Bell sound
34 Madame Karenina
35 New York, e.g., to Henri
37 Time-related
38 Blade sharpener
39 Author LeShan
40 55-Across has played many of these
43 Holder of 1,093 patents
45 He's a Wonder
46 On
47 Shows fear
* 50 Capri, for one
52 In any way
54 Winter blanket
56 A6 or TT
57 Not in harbor
58 Wit

by Elizabeth C. Gorski

ACROSS

1 Proj. begun in 1984
4 Kipling's wolf pack leader
9 In a fog
14 Shot spot
15 Charity allotments
16 Industrial Light and Magic creator
17 They're used in dumping
20 Dressing ingredient
21 Not be serious
22 In the thick of
23 Travel guide list
24 Tiny fraction of a foot-pound
26 Secret sharer
30 So
31 Quasimodo's job
* 32 A mint
33 "The Seduction of Joe Tynan" star
34 Architect Mies van der __
36 Sides in some wars
39 Hearty fare
43 They may be crushed
44 Worshipers' place
46 Fight figure
47 When Taanit Esther is observed
48 Subject preceder
49 Untouchable
53 Takes courses?
54 The 13 books from Romans to Philemon
56 Keeps an eye on figures?
* 57 Works with afterimages

58 Magritte's "Ceci n'est pas __ pipe"
59 "I'm stumped"
60 N.J. town on the Hudson
61 City grid: Abbr.

DOWN

1 Born loser
2 "You wish!"
3 Picture
4 Hot or cold, e.g.: Abbr.
5 Flake
6 K-12, in education
7 Kind of library
8 Not on the level?
9 Treble clef readers
10 1984 Peace Nobelist
11 Set back?
12 It catches some waves
13 Apuleius's "golden" one
18 Alerts
19 Coastal raptor
25 "Oh, wow!"
27 Reform targets
28 Carried out
29 Gasteyer of "Saturday Night Live"
30 Impractical person?
32 "Comin' __ the Rye"
34 Darling on the field
35 Stock page hdg.
36 One who makes a mark: Abbr.
37 Way back when
38 Like some divorces
39 Something seen
40 Growth ring
41 Treacherous type
42 They may be in a bun
44 Port near Ta'izz
45 Having as constituents
47 Surface
50 Mr. Miniver
51 It's 6.5 on the Mohs scale
52 Hide a mike on
54 Collectible cap
55 Marie, e.g.: Abbr.

by Harvey Estes and Nancy Salomon

ACROSS
1 Get comfy
7 They're obviously happy
14 Gave drills to
15 Ship-to-shore handler
* 16 Good way to rest
17 Monteverdi opera
18 Incentive to buy tickets
20 First name among sex symbols
21 "Tonight ___ Comes" (hit by the Cars)
22 Black
26 Grow every which way
* 30 It's like -like
32 Touch of frost
33 Whoosis
37 It may be fueled and driven
40 Like moonstones
41 Symbol of America
43 Emma player in "The Avengers"
44 Catch, so to speak
45 Cloverleaf part
49 Detection device
52 State since 1863: Abbr.
54 Gore Vidal's "Burr," e.g.
55 Cheap way to go
60 Item for a tyro on the slopes
63 Some roofs
64 Losing
65 It might be picked out
66 "With Reagan" author
67 Some N.S.A. employees

DOWN
1 "Huh-uh"
2 Kind of egg
3 Cottontail's tail
4 Archaic preposition
5 Actor ___ Cobb
6 They were written in Old Norse
7 Car halter
8 Frontier figure
9 Cry before taking off
10 Mazda model
11 No short time
12 Cartoon dog
13 Lady of Sp.
14 Composes
19 Sigma ___ (fraternity men)
23 ___ B'rith
24 Depict
25 It has a guarded tip
27 Grass bristles
28 "Wait just a minute!"
29 Lights
31 River resident
34 Create striking sentences?
35 Pitching coach Johnny
36 N.Y. Met, e.g.
37 They won't get off the ground
38 "Hot Diggity" singer
39 Mideast land
42 1889 Vice President ___ P. Morton
46 One who suspends an action, at law
47 Unlikely donors
48 Oater assemblage
50 Agatha Christie's "There Is ___"
51 First name in talk shows
53 Jellied garnish
56 They're picked in Hawaii
57 It's harvested in Hawaii
58 Doofus
59 Passing ___
60 Jazzman Koffman
61 Like some candidates: Abbr.
62 "Miss Saigon" setting

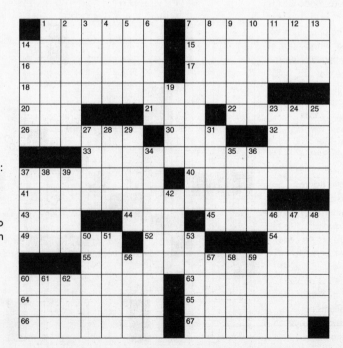

by Jim Page

ACROSS

1 Strikes among co-workers?
10 Overthrow, e.g.
15 Engineer's charge
16 Its capital is St.-Étienne
17 Really dresses down
18 It ends in a point
19 Lift, so to speak
20 Wizard's need
22 Managed
* 23 Article in Die Zeit
25 Fixed
26 Rooter's noise?
28 "Cool!"
31 Beverage suffix
32 It may be stolen
34 Stop along the Trans-Siberian Railroad
37 Traveling
39 American chicken variety
42 Soap scent
46 Guinea __
47 Put one's name on
49 Hawaiian harvest
50 Crate
53 Ball girl?
55 Hebrew for "day"
56 Flying Circus performer
59 Arises unexpectedly
61 Cell dissolution
62 Mottled mount
64 Balances
65 Stadiumgoer
66 Like some mountains
67 African danger

DOWN

1 Places for bières
2 Like 29-Down
3 "The Far Country" actress Calvet
* 4 You may be down on one
5 Eliminate one's shadow?
6 Wok concoction
7 __ Nova
8 Math makes up half of it: Abbr.
9 __ record
10 Short and sweet?
11 Criticize in no uncertain terms
12 Chicken breasts may come with it
13 "As You Like It" hero
14 One might do it after being stamped
21 African dangers
24 One acting on impulse?
27 Joined together
29 "Wellaway!"
30 Blotto
33 One way to travel: Abbr.
35 Cartoonist Keane
36 Fighting
38 Strained
39 Word after two, three or four
40 Eton's founder
41 Cut into
43 Lets go
44 Awakening
45 Guests
48 Take off
51 Breezing through
52 No bruiser
54 They have heads and threads
57 Definitive
58 Actor Omar
60 Prepare to be shot
63 His name is a letter short of his description

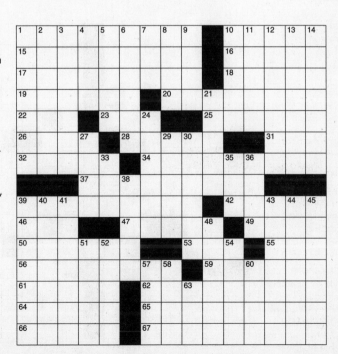

by Joe DiPietro

ACROSS

1 Like a tête-à-tête sofa
8 Drink to one's health
15 Reason to separate swine
16 Roadblock
17 Beat in a shootout
18 Charges
19 Short, in a way
20 1,500 years before the Wright brothers' first flight
21 Onetime club initials
22 70's–90's pitcher Charlie
25 Kind of coil
28 Rd. map line
30 "O Sanctissima," e.g.
32 Buff
33 Like coated fabrics
38 Went off the beam?
39 Gracious admission of an error
* 40 Spooky place?: Abbr.
41 Pivot
42 The buck stops here
43 Big name at Notre Dame
46 Clashing
48 Spot
51 Rays
53 Comparison
55 Style of Hals and Velázquez
57 Some newsbreaks
58 Flower cluster
59 Look through blinds, say
60 Changed
61 Subscription cards, e.g.

DOWN

1 Beat, in a way
2 Divert
3 Ensconced eatery
4 Robert of "Guys and Dolls"
5 Uses as a roost
6 Wordsworth's Muse
7 Bird that nests in chimneys
8 Unhealthy mix
9 Surrounded by
10 Problem in an alley
11 "Ogives" composer
12 Name in the middle of a masthead
* 13 "There ___ Mountain" (1967 Donovan hit)
14 Umpire's cry
23 Like much lost-and-found property
24 Has dates
26 Pierce
27 Chipped in
29 "Later!"
31 Unreliable source
33 Select on a computer
34 Cellist's cube
35 Intentions
36 Some winter merriment
37 Kind of shell
44 Connie's portrayer, in "The Godfather"

45 Order
47 Resort near the White River National Forest
49 Dweller on the Bering Sea
50 Conquers
52 Castaway's home
54 Fulfill, as a bid
55 Dashboard abbr.
56 ___ de vie
57 Big inits. in news

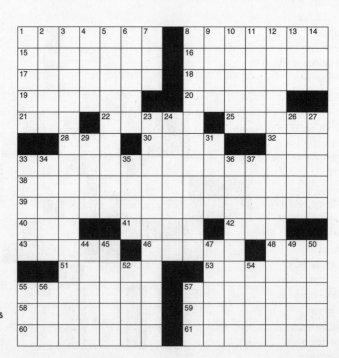

by Patrick D. Berry

ACROSS

1 Place for tired Turkish travelers
7 Liberal, in politics
15 41-Across request
16 Doctor, at times
17 American Shaker leader
18 No place for a rig
19 Seascape sights
20 Weasel
21 Prefix with cycle
22 City on the Hudson
23 Lacks
24 Kind of engr.
25 It may be hard to follow
26 Zoe's role in "Master Class"
*27 São Paulo has one
28 "There's no turning back now"
30 Summer stretch: Abbr.
31 Dates
32 Secretly
36 Like a bairn
37 Bullheaded one?
38 Crab apple and others
41 Where to work on the side
42 One on le trône
43 Sch. with tuition
44 Work stations
45 Abbr. on an invoice
46 Abbr. in a price
47 "___ again!"
48 Swamp sound
49 Gurkha conquest of 1768
51 One of the friends on "Friends"
52 Quarterbacks
53 Igneous rock
54 View from Aberdeen
55 Units of volume

DOWN

1 Perturbed
2 Ruling class
3 Kind of sac
4 Good news for an investor
5 They may be blue in the face
6 Place for a ring, perhaps
7 Passage
8 Queen City of the Rockies
9 Beethoven's "Eroica" is in it
10 Bulbous vegetable
11 Like some observations
12 "Coming Up for Air" novelist
13 Did a farm job
14 It sublimes at -109.26°F
20 Agra attire
23 Speeders make it
*24 Figure skating?
26 Entangles
27 Coach
29 Did a farm job
30 Baxter and others
32 They're heard in a pen
33 Beam's path
34 Like Yogi Berra
35 Party favors
37 Title first awarded in 1952
38 Gain, as weight
39 6 × 9-inch book size
40 Boxer's trainer, e.g.
41 Political analyst Myers
44 Buggy places?
45 Came up
47 More than scrape
48 On-line activity
50 "Rocky III" actor
51 Where to find Charlie Rose

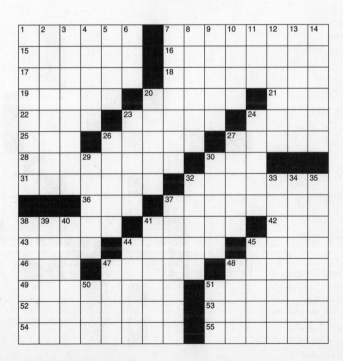

by Elizabeth C. Gorski

ACROSS

1 Reviewed
10 Colorful squawker
15 Where the Wildcats play
16 Building material
17 Like some immunological agents
18 Join securely
19 Pour __
20 Cordwood measure
22 He was well-preserved
23 1941 Oscar-winner Crisp
26 Oil source
27 First N.L.'er to hit 500 homers
28 Late risers
31 Mysterious visitor
32 Like some decisions
35 Interest, slangily
36 Free from limits
37 Great leveler
38 Allotment
39 Like some decisions
40 On the same page, so to speak
42 Pro __
43 Ready to deliver?
44 Abbr. on a gauge
* 45 Follower of "Rocky" or "Superman"
46 Unfair hiring
50 Invoice amount
51 Cause of some stomachaches
54 It may be skipped
55 Napoleons' relatives
57 Alienates
60 At attention
61 Protect from bugs
62 Wave catcher?
63 It helps you take off the top

DOWN

1 Place for a ribbon
2 Total
3 Author Sinclair
4 Painful piercing
5 Hardly a nymph
6 "__ he drove out of sight . . ."
7 Wolves' creations
8 Graduation mark
9 Bellwether
10 Reading buddies?
11 Cooler cooler
12 Like some seats
13 One-eighty
14 Retired
21 Was contingent (on)
24 Favor one side?
25 Opus __ (work of God)
29 Protection from bugs
30 Swindle
* 32 More than want
33 Half a noted comedy duo
34 Played tag, e.g.
35 Mixer
38 Striking sound
40 Of the flock
41 Frank's third
43 Misinforms
47 Buffalo Bill, e.g.
48 Avalanche
49 Nicholas who wrote "The Seven-Per-Cent Solution"
52 Isabel Allende's "Eva __"
53 Smooth
56 Big inits. in cable
58 Kind of mil. club
59 Eat

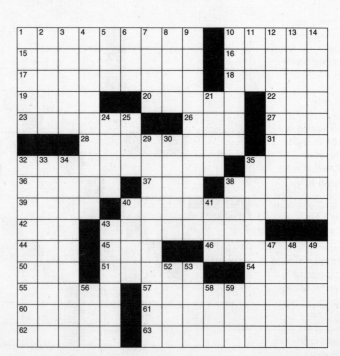

by Joe DiPietro

ACROSS

1 High-calorie treat *
16 London stage
17 Things on a cutting room floor?
18 "___ Not Dressing" (Crosby comedy)
19 Kind of shell
20 Byron's "___ to Napoleon Buonaparte"
21 Comment with a wrist-slap
22 Director Craven
24 Andrea ___ (ill-fated ship)
28 "Destination" in a 1950 sci-fi film
30 Conversation fillers
33 Roots
35 Strict disciplinarian
37 Country club?
39 Ice Age roamer
40 Dress
41 "Forty Modern Fables" writer
42 River feature
43 Bushes can be found here
44 Francis Drake, for one
45 Brand
48 Do doilies
50 Dictator Mobutu ___ Seko
51 "A God in Ruins" novelist
55 Guardianship
* 59 Literary figure?
60 Postprandial speakers

DOWN

1 Exult
2 "A waking dream": Aristotle
3 ___ and terminer (criminal court)
4 Meticulousness
5 Slangy 50's suffix
6 This might cause you to scratch
7 Like some colonies
8 Biggest-grossing film of 1956, with "The"
9 Logician's word
10 Have a date?
11 Tea, on the Thames
12 Western wolves
13 New Year's Eve adjective
14 "Gotcha"
15 Lo-___
21 Safari-goer's starting point
22 Unfavorable prognosis
23 International agreement
24 Ism
25 Mountain nymph
26 Dentist's direction
27 "___ Weak" (1988 Belinda Carlisle hit)
29 Grp. founded in Bogotá
30 Open, in a way
31 Singer Moore
32 Eyelid inflammations
34 2000 presidential candidate
36 Hungary's Nagy
38 First name in horror
44 Rows
46 Of ___ (so to speak)
47 Mideast drink made from fermented milk
48 Completely, after "in"
49 On a crossing
50 Turns at the Met
51 Items in niches
52 Bearskins, maybe
53 "This scepter'd ___" (England)
54 French honorees: Abbr.
55 Honeybun
56 Shell filler
57 Cartesian conclusion
58 ___ kwon do

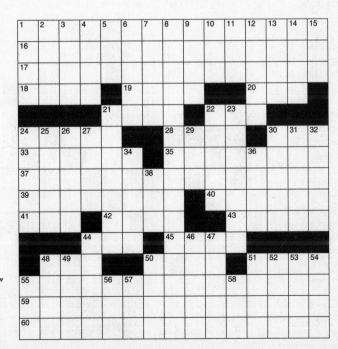

by Martin Ashwood-Smith

ACROSS
1 Persian War participant
7 It may take a beating
13 Pillars of the community
14 Film critic Kael
15 Wind god
16 Like some stomachs
17 Rattle of a sort
18 National competitor
19 Claustrophobic patient's dread
20 Siren
22 Make snaps, say
23 Sled parts
* 24 Comparatively cockeyed
25 Mass communication?
27 Flu symptom
28 It's a wrap
29 Playground equipment
30 Swallow
31 Like some pie crusts
32 If-___ (computer routines)
33 Popular supermarket tabloid
34 "___ sorry . . ."
35 Desire in the offing?
39 Mathematician Lovelace
40 Preener, perhaps
41 Made a pig of oneself?
43 Guardian
45 Loosen, as a 37-Down
46 Big rolls
47 Boil
48 Grayish green
49 Treasure

DOWN
1 Place vulnerable to ripping
2 They're entered in court
3 Like loads
4 Become less gripping?
5 Gas station plazas
6 Attacker
7 It holds water
8 Causes of some spinning wheels
9 Philip Roth's "___, the Fanatic"
10 Sent flying?
* 11 Does some shoal searching?
12 "The Alchemist" painter
14 Makes concrete?
16 Malicious
21 Punch
22 One given away
24 Sancerre and Sylvaner
25 Tears
26 Memorable 1999 hurricane
27 19th hole
28 It's full of 29-Downs
29 See 28-Down
30 Prominent 1988 Bush campaign adviser
31 Like some pie crusts
33 Subjects of ratios
35 Country singer Carter
36 Small fjord
37 It may have a blade
38 "Psycho" co-star, 1998
40 Ran
42 Believe
44 Early evictee

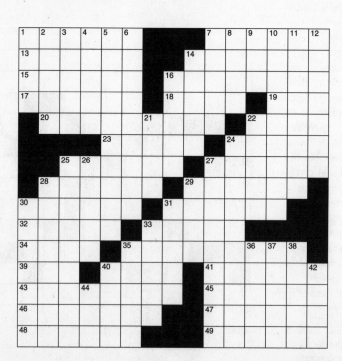

by Brendan Emmett Quigley

ACROSS

1 It's cut and dried
10 Parts of faiths
15 Uncompromising offer
16 Spirit
17 They're rarely hits
18 Uncanny
19 Some officers
20 Held
22 Fitting
23 Infuriate
24 Pearl Buck heroine
25 Renfrew's org., in old radio
26 Ticker locale: Abbr.
28 Title girl in a 1968 Buckinghams hit
29 Projection
30 Delicacy
32 Starts an occupation
34 Court figure
37 Some gang members
*38 Swordsman's belt worn diagonally from shoulder to hip
40 One of the Muppets
41 Seeing trouble
42 Kind of tag
44 Fictional hunter
48 Peculiarities
49 Picks (up)
50 Test in coll., perhaps
51 Delicacy
52 Heavy metal
54 Honoree's locale
55 Tear open
57 Set aside
59 ___-et-Loire (French department)
60 Takes care of

61 With 28-Down, newswoman who founded a college in Claremont, Calif.
62 Final, maybe

DOWN

1 English navigator who searched for the Northwest Passage
2 Queen of fiction
3 Passes over
4 Swells
5 Some sons
6 English author Blyton
7 Endured
8 Gets down
9 Polite response
10 Slough
11 Letters on a pump, maybe
12 Sales rep's accessory
13 Ancient magistrate
14 Gets more arduous, in a way
21 Dignify
25 Exude
27 Debussy's "Douze ___"
28 See 61-Across
31 Bubbly beginning?
33 Dash
34 Deep
35 Thinking
36 Sweetening agent
39 Shift
40 Ices

43 Conjectures
45 Lorre's "Casablanca" role
46 Offensive actions
47 Barren
52 Exposed
53 City on the Salt River
54 Nimble
*56 Chemical suffix
58 For instance

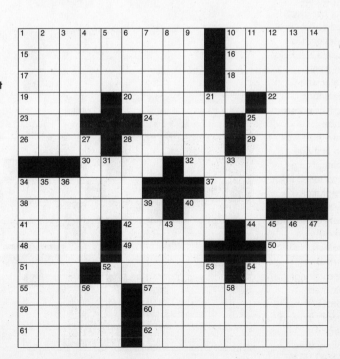

by Rich Norris

ACROSS

1 Permits passage, perhaps
11 Time of a famous dispatch
15 Bills
16 Custom officer's cry
17 Better
18 Stoic philosopher
19 Basket alternative
*20 Band with the album "Monster"
21 Singer Artis Ivey, familiarly
23 Physics class topic
24 Tape, say
26 Photocopied
30 It may follow one's convictions
31 Act starter
32 Not get used
33 Fast cars
34 "Mystery Date" actress ___ Polo
36 Innocent
39 Prefix with centenary
42 1980's program: Abbr.
44 Early Bird was the first one
48 Rating range
51 Long-tailed finch
52 Desolation
54 "Catch-22" pilot
55 Mezzo Berganza
56 Hikes
58 Brothers
59 Purlieu
60 It has strings attached
63 Force
64 There's no end to them
65 "Show Boat" cap'n
66 Casting aid

DOWN

1 Thumbs strike them
2 Fort Lauderdale suburb
3 Table centerpiece
4 Barrage
5 Indian name starter
6 Picasso's love
7 More likely to erupt
8 Chaotic
9 P.D. figure
10 Speaker's asset
11 Needing to be cracked?
12 Casino activity
13 Like ground sloths
14 Old comics
22 Bit for the silent butler
25 Overlay with wood or plaster
27 Peter Jennings's birthplace: Abbr.
28 Toll
*29 Peter, Paul and Mary
35 Starting point for Pasteur
37 Barn sound
38 Upscale wheels
39 Fiesta fare
40 Join, redundantly
41 Hit, in a way
43 John Hancock, e.g.
45 Shrimp
46 Does an aquarium job
47 Least long
49 Compact
50 Accepts
53 Place for a finial
57 Sound amount
58 Boba ___ of "Star Wars"
61 Flight coordinators: Abbr.
62 Miller's lover in "Henry & June"

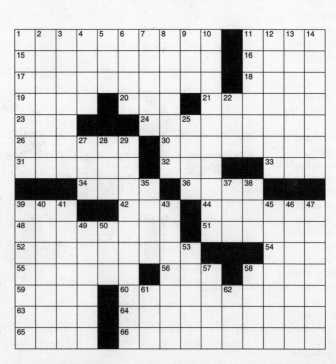

by Nancy Joline

ACROSS

1 Bygone hangout for 64-Acrosses
9 Popular money-raiser
15 Regional figure
16 Joined forces?
17 Common restaurant request
18 Lights-out activity
19 Post-graduate pursuit
20 Part of some military academy attire
22 ___ cheese
24 "Well . . . ?"
25 Scheme
27 Old African rulers
* 28 It won't keep you up
30 Steady
31 Stumped
33 ___ Flite (bicycle brand)
35 Untested
36 Family gathering, maybe
40 Bill provider
41 Touristy district
42 ___ Miguel
43 California city, county or river
45 Blockish
47 Head of the Egyptian god Thoth
51 Walk noisily
53 Big time
54 Peace Nobelist Cassin
55 Symbol of speed
59 Grey who co-starred in "Three Smart Girls"
60 Defensive wall around an outer court of a castle
61 Lighter?
63 Confine

64 See 1-Across and 2-Down
65 African carrier
66 Employer for creative types

DOWN

1 Like many packages
2 Modern hangout for 64-Acrosses
3 Latitude
4 Shooter
* 5 Defraud
6 Réception V.I.P.
7 City southwest of Midland
8 The groom's ex, say
9 Literally, "scraped"
10 Smart ones

11 Screwballs
12 Adjust
13 Docent
14 Suffix on some country names
21 Played a card?
23 Certain N.C.O.
26 Collection area
28 Endured
29 Spring up
32 Some E.R. admissions
34 Bob Dylan's "___ Night Like This"
36 War of the Roses battle site
37 Blunt, perhaps
38 Bearded growth
39 Film follower
40 Like some history: Abbr.
44 Fetish

46 Get really hot
48 Favorable
49 Very soon
50 Halter?
52 Aristocrats
56 Scot's "since"
57 Not docked
58 Big ape
60 Was taken in
62 Response from a bonny lass?

by Rich Norris

ACROSS

* **1** It has two bands
10 Some screamers
14 Religious
15 Kind of race
16 Law firm hotshot
17 Prefix on names of durable products
18 With 55-Down, where to be quiet?
19 Certain newspaper writer
21 N.S. clock setting
* **22** Verdi's "Fu la sorte dell' armi," e.g.
25 Pack up
26 It may be loaded
27 One who takes things back, in old lingo
29 When arguments begin?
31 Some M.I.T. grads
32 Year of Philip I's birth
33 Sewer lines?
35 PC program
37 Put on a pedestal
41 "The Mod Squad" co-star
43 ___ Dashan (highest point in Ethiopia)
45 Like royal descent, usually
46 Traces
47 Oils and such
48 Hue duller than heliotrope
50 Where a 19-Across may sit
52 Salsa singer Cruz
53 It keeps the bugs out
56 Get down in church

57 The New Yorker contributor until 1968
58 Criteria: Abbr.
59 They may be false

DOWN

1 Not at home, perhaps
2 Isn't kidding
3 Hummingbird, e.g.
4 Chi follower
5 Skill-building
6 Clark's "Mogambo" co-star
7 Cartoonist Browne
8 It may be hard to overcome
9 Grimm figure
10 Most like a cumulus cloud
11 Broadcasting unit?
12 Tough opponents
13 Web, at times
15 Mimetic behavior
20 Like most modern furniture
23 Dull
24 Swirled
28 Phidias subject
30 Confession collection
34 Wipe out
35 Sustenance
36 Covered, in a way
38 Less frowzy
39 School stock

40 An original Mouseketeer
41 Old telegraph machine sounds
42 1986 Indy winner
44 Obsolescent office positions
49 1999 N.F.L. Defensive Player of the Year
51 1980 combatant
54 Itinerary abbr.
55 See 18-Across

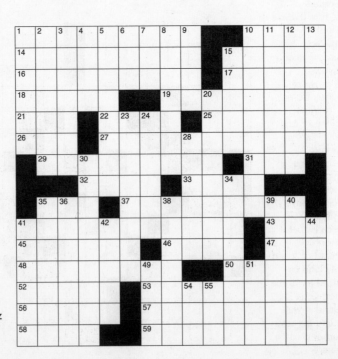

by Randolph Ross

ACROSS

* 1 In other words
* *** 7** Ally on TV
* 14 Plain
* 15 Like some fine pottery
* 16 PANT
* 17 CHEF
* 18 Lively folk dance
* 19 Expensive car trips
* 20 One of four Holy Roman emperors
* 21 Surface
* 23 Scandinavian money
* 24 Some nods
* 25 Jazz composer Evans
* 26 SPED
* 28 Coins with profiles of Nehru
* 31 Having no bounds: Abbr.
* 32 Pop music's Hanson, e.g.
* 34 Vote in Québec
* *** 35** Traits helpful in answering the eight capitalized clues
* 41 ". . . ___ will!"
* 42 City on the Rhein
* 43 Fuzziness
* 44 Kind of case
* 47 MOST
* 48 Windy City transportation inits.
* 49 48-Across's specialty
* 50 What some surrogates get
* 52 Air beyond the clouds
* 54 1970's Vogue discovery
* 55 Name for an Irish lass
* 56 River known in ancient times as Obringa
* 57 DEFY
* 59 RUNS
* 61 Strikeouts?
* 62 High point
* 63 Curtain decoration
* 64 Like the worst predictions

DOWN

* 1 Place for diplomacy
* 2 Eulogist's activity
* 3 City that's the title of an Emmylou Harris song
* 4 Melodic subjects
* 5 Suffix with project
* 6 Lang. unit
* 7 Braggart
* 8 Sights
* 9 ___ Day (May 1, in Hawaii)
* 10 NAVE
* 11 David, e.g.
* 12 Rouen relations
* 13 Concert voices
* 15 Quality
* 19 Specifically
* 22 Glycerides, e.g.
* 27 1970's sitcom
* 29 Result of some arm-twisting?
* 30 ___ Claire (city near Montreal)
* 33 Where Mork and Mindy honeymooned
* 36 POSE
* 37 Herbert Hoover, for one
* 38 Responsible
* 39 Bistros and the like
* 40 Gaunt
* 44 Land development
* 45 Rain forest sights
* 46 Just desserts
* 49 Transfix
* 51 Struggles
* 53 Accompaniment for a fife
* 55 Title meaning "chieftain"
* 58 Wish nullified
* 59 Pop
* 60 Prefix with grammatical

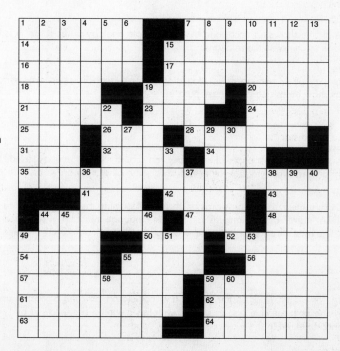

by David J. Kahn

HINTS AND TIPS

Puzzle 1

26-Across
Fill-in-the-blank clues are often the simplest and most straightforward ones to answer. Start with these (or other answers you're sure of) and build from there.

44-Across
Many fill-in-the-blank clues provide additional information in parentheses, such as a word or phrase that is synonymous with the phrase containing the blank.

Puzzle 2

23-Across
Clues and answers always agree in number, meaning that if a clue is plural, the answer must also be plural (not necessarily, of course, always ending in -S).

42-Across
When a clue calls for a verb as an answer, the two must agree both in tense and number. For example, if the clue is in the present tense, third-person singular, the answer must be in the same form.

Puzzle 3

1-Down
This type of clue shows up occasionally. It is a simple analogy of the form "A is to B as C is to D." Fill in the blank to complete the relationship.

50-Down
Very often a clue is nothing more than a straightforward, dictionary-type synonym. Precise, helpful synonyms show up frequently in easy puzzles.

Puzzle 4

23-Across
When a question mark appears after a clue, you should expect the unexpected. The answer will not be a straightforward synonym, but rather a pun or some other play on words.

41-Down
Answers are sometimes foreign words or phrases. Assuming the foreign term has not been adopted into English (like "naive" or "per annum"), a foreign-language indicator of some sort will always appear in the clue. The most direct such indicator is a tag like "Lat.," "Fr.," "Sp.," or "Ger."

Puzzle 5

67-Across
The word "on" is provided in the clue to give context on how the answer is used. In other words, in everyday use both the clue and its answer with this meaning are followed by "on." Other words commonly parenthesized in this way are "for," "to," and "in."

60-Down
Sometimes a clue is a fill-in-the-blank in disguise. A word like "starter," "beginner," "opener," "intro,"

or "lead-in" may signal you to think of a word (the answer) that can precede the given word to complete a common phrase.

Puzzle 6

62-Across
The "e.g." tag (Latin for "exempli gratia") indicates that the item named in the clue is an example of a general category. You're supposed to say what it is an example of. This tag may also appear spelled out as "for example," "for instance," or "for one."

21-Down
"In England" is a straightforward way to indicate that the answer is a British term or spelling. (Hint for Canadian solvers: The answer here is also used in Canada.)

Puzzle 7

1-Across
If a word that is not usually abbreviated appears in abbreviated form in the clue (like "Dept." for "Department"), then it's a signal that the answer is also abbreviated.

33-Down
"Kind of" at the beginning of a clue can literally mean a kind or variety of something (for example, "Kind of cat" for SIAMESE). Often, though, it merely acts as a disguised fill-in-the-blank signal (for example, "Kind of ticket" for MEAL; a "meal" is not really a kind of ticket, but "meal ticket" is a common phrase).

Puzzle 8

53-Across
The word "partner" in a clue is a way of asking you to think of a word that commonly goes with another word to make a common phrase with "and" in the middle. For example, "Shaker's partner" could be MOVER (as in "mover and shaker") and "Rough's partner" could be TUMBLE.

50-Down
Sometimes when a proper name is asked for, there is ambiguity as to whether the given name is a first or last name. Try to be open to either possibility.

Puzzle 9

26-Down
Keep in mind that an answer may be a phrase rather than a single word—and in *New York Times* crosswords there are no hints like "2 wds." and "3 wds." to help you. Figuring out which answers are phrases is part of the puzzle.

44-Down
If a clue is in the form of an adjective, it must have an adjective as an answer. Clues that start with "like" very often call for adjectival answers.

Puzzle 10

1-Across
The word "competitor" is a signal for you to think of a competing company or brand for the one given in the clue. Other common signals of this type are "rival," "alternative," and "shelfmate."

61-Down
When a clue consists of a common expression in quotes, it usually means you're to think of another common expression with the same meaning from spoken English.

Puzzle 11

6-Down
A tag like "briefly" or "for short" in a clue means that the answer is a familiar shortened form of a word or phrase—like "moc" for "moccasin" or "Indy" for "Indianapolis." This signal will never be used for abbreviations that appear only in writing (like "jct" for "junction"), which need a more traditional abbreviation signal.

58-Down
This indicates that the answer is usually, or in some cases must be, followed by the word "up" in order to substitute for the word in the clue.

Puzzle 12

37-Across
This type of clue asks you to identify what one of the letters in an abbreviation stands for. In *Times* crosswords, the answer to a clue like this will always be fully spelled out, unless there is also an "Abbr." tag. For example, "The 'A' in P.G.A." would be answered ASSOCIATION, not ASSN.

60-Across
When a name appears after a colon in a clue, this identifies the source of the clue's quotation.

Puzzle 13

27-Across
Some clues are either-you-know-it-or-you-don't facts or bits of trivia. If you're sure you don't know it, you'll have to arrive at the answer by completing the crossing words.

18-Down
Clues that start with "more" are almost always answered by the comparative form of an adjective, and thus end in -ER.

Puzzle 14

5-Across
In some cases a clue may be asking for either a verb or an adjective, depending on how it's read. Stay mentally flexible.

27-Down
If a clue is in quotes, it may signify that its supposed truthfulness is based on an adage, song title, lyric, or other subjective source.

Puzzle 15

34-Down
Occasionally an entire clue will be in a foreign language. This is another way to indicate that the answer will be a word or phrase in that same language.

49-Down
Fill-in-the-blank clues are not always easy. Sometimes several different potential answers may fit, and in harder puzzles this ambiguity may be intentional.

Puzzle 16

46-Across
In clues listing two or more examples of a category (in which you're to identify the category), the usual tag "e.g." or "for one" may be omitted.

37-Down
Another way to indicate a foreign word is to use a first or last name in the clue that a person who speaks that language might have. Here, for example, you're supposed to provide the Spanish word for "that."

Puzzle 17

36-Across

Sometimes a puzzle will contain an explanation of its theme via a special entry in the grid. This may be done in cases where the theme is particularly subtle and an extra hint may be useful to solvers . . . or simply because the bonus answer is amusing. (Note that the daily *New York Times* crosswords do not have titles in the newspaper. The titles on these puzzles were added especially for this book.)

40-Down

Many clues utilize this "as" format to give the solver more helpful and specific information as to how the clue-and-answer combination work together.

Puzzle 18

2-Down

When a clue references another, you can place either the referenced clue or its answer into the original clue to get the intended reading.

39-Down

The answer is a word that one of the abbreviation's letters stands for (that is, Q, E, or D). This is like a clue that reads, say, "The 'E' of Q.E.D.," only less specific.

Puzzle 19

8-Down

The "Var." tag stands for "variant." The answer will be a spelling or version of a word that's much less common than the usual—although still sanctioned by at least one major American dictionary.

11-Down

Clues that begin with "maximally" almost always indicate the superlative form of an adjective and therefore will usually end in -EST.

Puzzle 20

47-Across

"In a way" is a very common tag in clues, asking the solver to think of one way in which the clue might be true. For example, Mardi Gras may be celebrated in many different ways. The answer means "celebrated Mardi Gras" in a particular way.

57-Down

Clues of this format usually indicate an alphabetical sequence—namely, the letters that appear between the two given letters. The words "link" and "connection" are other commonly used indicators of this sort.

Puzzle 21

9-Across

Because the first word in a clue is capitalized regardless of whether or not it is a proper noun, capital-ization can be misleading, often purposefully. A word that may appear to be common may, in fact, be

a proper noun.

25-Down

A clue that begins with "how" usually signals an adverbial answer. While an adverb usually ends in -LY, it doesn't necessarily do so—nor is it necessarily a single word.

Puzzle 22

1-Across

A plural answer may be disguised in a clue in various ways. The use of "trio," "quartet," etc., is one method.

53-Down
When a clue asks for a person's name without offering a first or last name as a help, the answer will always be the person's last name or else the first and last name together, but never the first name only.

Puzzle 23

41-Down
In this common clue format, "ending" is simply another way to say "suffix."

59-Down
When two surnames are listed, look for a first name that's shared by the two famous people.

Puzzle 24

62-Across
When a character's last name is given in a clue and you're seeking the actor who played a particular role, the answer is parallel—that is, usually a last name also. The same would be true of first names.

7-Down
Clues of the form "[abbreviation] part" are often just shorthand for the more standard "Part of [abbreviation]."

Puzzle 25

42-Down
The word "like" suggests that the answer is an adjective that can describe the thing named.

53-Down
The tags "maybe" and "perhaps" generally signal that only in some instances or circumstances will the clue match its answer.

Puzzle 26

31-Across
Similar to the word "more" (see hint to puzzle #13, 18-Down), clues starting with "less" usually are answered by comparative adjectives ending in -ER.

65-Across
This is another way to mask a plural answer.

Puzzle 27

15-Across
When thinking of possible answers, apply the "substitution test": Use the clue phrase in a sentence, then think of other words or phrases that could substitute for it exactly, both grammatically and in meaning.

26-Down
Tags like "they say" and "supposedly" signal that the answer is not an undisputed fact, but is controversial or debatable, or may be part of a common adage.

Puzzle 28

50-Across
A clue asking for a date is usually answered by a year in Roman numerals. The standard Roman numerals are: I = 1, V = 5, X = 10, L = 50, C = 100, D = 500, M = 1,000. (For the rules of forming Roman numerals, check an encyclopedia or other reference.)

38-Down
In clues, abbreviations that are generally written as abbreviations in everyday writing (for example, "Sen." in front of a person's name) should not be interpreted as signaling an abbreviated answer. Only an abbreviation for a word that is usually spelled out is an abbreviation signal.

Puzzle 29

51-Across
This common clue form asks you to think of a noun that is often preceded or described by the adjective in the clue.

8-Down
A clue that starts with "some" is usually answered by a plural noun. The answer is a general category of things described in the clue.

Puzzle 30

20-Across
Question marks in theme clues (that is, clues for a puzzle's longest answers) usually mean something different from what they do in normal clues. Often a theme answer is a made-up phrase, and the clue's question mark signals this fact, even though the clue itself may be a literal definition of the contrived answer.

35-Across
In clues of this format, you're given a certain number of something in a set, but the set itself is not named—and therefore must be mentally supplied.

Puzzle 31

4-Down
The hyphen here indicates a word part to which a prefix can be added to form a regular word. The answer has nothing to do with word "pod" per se, which is why it's preceded by a hyphen.

61-Down
Often "ending" or "ender" indicates that you're looking for a suffix that can be added to the given word to form a new word.

Puzzle 32

31-Across
Consider all possible meanings of a clue, including uses in different parts of speech. The clue "Sound" is tricky, because "sound" means different things as a noun, verb, and adjective.

10-Down
In most cases, a clue that starts with an "-ing" verb will be answered by an "-ing" verb. But keep in mind that such words can also be gerunds, which function as nouns. For example, the clue "Taking out the trash, e.g." might be answered by CHORE.

Puzzle 33

14-Across
The word "cousin" in a clue is usually a signal to look for another creature or a thing that is related, either literally or figuratively, to whatever the clue says.

18-Down
Partly for space-saving reasons, crossword clues tend to be succinct. This two-word clue is just a short way of saying "A heroic character in a Leon Uris novel."

Puzzle 34

1-Across
When a clue uses very informal or slangy language, the answer will also be informal or slangy.

11-Down
"Leader" is another common (if deceptive) way of asking you to think of a word (the answer) that can be added to the beginning of a given word to form a new word. This usage may or may not be tipped off by a question mark, depending on the overall difficulty of the puzzle.

Puzzle 35

56-Across
"Equipment" is one of those ambiguous words that can be fairly answered by either a singular or plural noun. "Gear" is another.

47-Down
On first reading, it's not clear what the clue means. The answer might refer to either the first "it" or the second—or both. It does help to realize that "out of it" is an idiomatic phrase.

Puzzle 36

50-Across
In this common clue type, "dir." stands for "direction," and the answer will be a compass-point abbreviation like ENE, ESE, SSW, etc.

58-Down
The word "connector" or "connection" may disguise a fill-in-the-blank clue. What word or words can "connect" the two given words to complete a common phrase?

Puzzle 37

3-Down
Any clue that ends with "again" or "anew" is likely to have an answer starting with RE-.

32-Down
When a clue contains a Roman numeral and requires some form of mathematical calculation, the answer will always be another Roman numeral. (See the hint to puzzle #28, 50-Across.)

Puzzle 38

28-Across
This clue and its theme-mates elsewhere in the puzzle are a little vague. Think of all the things a "work" might be—for example, a literary, dramatic, musical or art work.

3-Down
Since the clue contains the French spelling of "Napoleon" (with an accent over the "é"), look for a French word that would describe Elba.

Puzzle 39

1-Down
Sometimes "center" or "middle," when used in this way, is to be interpreted as "word or words that may appear in the center."

60-Down
In this two-step clue, you should first figure out what the abbreviated letters stand for and then determine what they're examples of.

Puzzle 40

51-Across
If you've figured out what the theme answers at 20- and 36-Across have in common, you'll have a big leg up on getting 51-Across, too (whether or not you're familiar with the song).

53-Down
An "angel" can be a heavenly being, a well-behaved child, or a backer of a theatrical production. Think about the third meaning for this clue.

Puzzle 41

15-Across
The clue is a sneaky way of asking you for a prefix meaning "a lot."

13-Down
Here, a vital piece of missing information must be inferred—namely, what activity is being referred to? Figuring this out may give you a nice "aha!" feeling.

Puzzle 42

12-Down
Because the tag "for example" is rendered here in Spanish, the answer will also be Spanish.

38-Down
An alphabet trio is simply three successive letters of the alphabet. Similar clues are "Alphabet run," "Alphabet lineup," "Telephone trio" (for any series of letters on a telephone dial), etc.

Puzzle 43

17-Across
As with the hint to puzzle #41, 13-Down, vital information is missing here. Billions of "what"? This information must be supplied by the solver.

55-Down
"Book after," "Book before," etc, in the absence of any other information, almost always refer to books of the Bible.

Puzzle 44

39-Down
This clue asks you for the plural of a person's name—a famous person named King and others who share King's first name.

59-Down
Bear in mind that the verb "can't" in a clue can lead to either a third-person singular or plural answer. For example, "He [can't stand] broccoli" substitutes for "He [HATES] broccoli," while "They [can't stand] broccoli" substitutes for "They [HATE] broccoli" (no -S).

Puzzle 45

32-Across
Note the absence of a comma after "Add," which greatly affects the clue's meaning.

51-Down
As puzzles increase in difficulty, clues that might otherwise end in a question mark may not, depending on how literally the clue can be interpreted.

Puzzle 46

44-Across
When a clue says "word with [something]," the answer may either precede or follow the words given in the clue to complete familiar phrases. By tradition, the answer will either precede both words in the clue or follow both words in the clue, but not precede one and follow the other.

12-Down
Words that are spelled the same but pronounced differently are sometimes used ambiguously. For example, "number" may be a numerical digit or something that numbs. (In this clue, it's probably obvious which kind of "shower" is intended.)

Puzzle 47

20-Across

If you're certain that an answer is right, but there doesn't seem to be enough squares to write it in, you may need to insert more than one letter in one of the squares—or even draw a little symbol or picture in a certain square. This will be part of the puzzle's theme, working both across and down, and is likely to be repeated elsewhere in the grid.

39-Across

In this case, had a mere comma been placed after the word "one," the question mark might not have been needed.

Puzzle 48

41-Across

If a clue starts "Like . . ." and is followed by a musical work, the answer usually describes the musical key in which the piece was written.

4-Down

Think not only of a word that could potentially precede and follow "in," but one that could occupy both positions at the same time to form a familiar three-word phrase.

Puzzle 49

13-Down

Irregular verbs like "put" and "set" can be tricky, because the answer is just as likely to be in the past tense as in the present.

50-Down

Typically, when a clue begins "First name in . . . ," the answer is an unusual first name (like ERLE) that is associated with a particular famous person (e.g., mystery writer Erle Stanley Gardner) and that would be too easily guessed if the last name were given outright.

Puzzle 50

15-Across

The fact that the clue ends in a question mark is a strong indication that the answer has nothing to do with romance.

30-Down

Some obscurish words, particularly ones that are short and vowel-heavy, show up in crosswords much more often than they do in everyday speech and writing. This is one of these words. If you can memorize, say, several hundred of these used most often in crosswords, you will quickly become a much better solver.

Puzzle 51

25-Across

Fortunately, only one note on the musical scale is spelled with three letters, so solving this clue is much easier than if it had said "Scale tones."

30-Down

In the house style of The New York Times, names of plays, books, films, TV shows, comic strips, etc., are generally spelled with quotation marks, while the names of games, ships, newspapers, magazines, and reference works aren't signaled in any way other than capitalization. Since "Othello" here has quotation marks, the clue must refer to the play, not the character in it or the popular board game of the same name.

Puzzle 52

20-Across
Some puzzles' themes are quite tricky. You'll have to be imaginative to figure out what's going on in this one. The unusual device in 20-Across is repeated in 33-, 39-, and 48-Across.

47-Down
The tag "so to speak" usually indicates that the word or phrase in the clue is slangy or idiomatic, while the answer is not.

Puzzle 53

15-Across
The clue "Regarding" for a four-letter answer is almost always IN RE or AS TO. You have to solve one of the crossing words to find out which is correct.

58-Down
A "court" can be either a judicial court, a sports court (basketball or otherwise), or a palace court. To discover which one is meant by the clue, you'll (again) need some letters from crossing answers.

Puzzle 54

14-Across
The puzzlemaker and editor are being tricky here. Don't assume the answer is a thing or place.

21-Down
Not every plural answer ends in an -S.

Puzzle 55

46-Across
The use of old hipster talk ("man!") in the clue signals that the answer will involve an expression of the same sort.

54-Down
If a common idiom ends in a question mark, it's almost certain that the answer will not refer to its usual idiomatic meaning, but rather a literal interpretation of the words.

Puzzle 56

19-Down
While verbs in the past tense usually end in -ED, they don't always do so. This is one of these exceptions.

58-Down
The word "letters" here signals, in a sly way, that the answer is an abbreviation (composed of "letters") that's related to news.

Puzzle 57

1-Down
The word "place," "locale," or "site" in a clue is often ambiguous. It can mean the place where something is located or a location within the thing named.

46-Down
When a word like "itself" here is in quotes, it may be the English translation of a word in a common foreign phrase. In this case, no further hint is given as to what particular language the phrase is in.

Puzzle 58

56-Across
In many modern crosswords, like those in *The New York Times,* you can expect many multiword answers. These include phrases that are common in everyday speech but not listed in a dictionary.

13-Down
This clue is the same as the one for 27-Across but has a completely different answer. Consider that "OK" can be either a verb or an adjective.

Puzzle 59

18-Across
In crossword puzzles, letters of the alphabet are sometimes spelled out—like ESS for S, ELL for L, WYE for Y, etc.

32- and 33-Down
This is a common answer-linking technique. The answers to the two clues together make a phrase entered at 33- and 32-Down, in that order.

Puzzle 60

12-Down
This is a useful name to remember. It will probably show up in crosswords for years to come—long after the news it's based upon has faded from memory.

51-Down
Be aware that numbers in crosswords (1, 2, 3, etc.) can be spelled out in letters. There is a spelled-out number in this answer.

Puzzle 61

5-Across
As puzzles increase in difficulty, clues that otherwise might end in question marks may not use them if the reading of the clue is literal enough.

49-Down
Here is an unusual example of a starting word that is almost always an adverb or adjective being used trickily as a verb.

Puzzle 62

17-Across
In an easier puzzle, this same clue would probably be more helpful either by being enclosed in quotes or having a "so to speak" tag attached.

50-Down
Because the name Capri is spelled the same in both its native Italian as well as in English, the answer may be in either language.

Puzzle 63

32-Across
The articles "a" and "the" are usually missing from the starts of clues. When "a," for example, does appear before a noun in this way, you can interpret it as "one example of a" or "a certain."

57-Across
This is doubly sly: First, the part of speech of the first word is ambiguous. Second, the plural that is called for doesn't necessarily lead to an answer ending in -S.

Puzzle 64

16-Across
Clues that begin "Good way to," "One way to," or "Way to" usually indicate that the answer is an adverb. It doesn't necessarily end in -LY, however.

30-Across
This strange-looking clue should be interpreted as "This suffix is similar to the suffix '-like'."

Puzzle 65

23-Across
The clue "Article in [name of foreign publication]" almost always leads to a foreign word for "a" or "the." In this case the language is German.

4-Down
Don't think of "one" here as in "one of these," but rather as a definite number. For example, the clue "A cola may have one" could be answered by CALORIE.

Puzzle 66

40-Across
An occasional feature of tricky clues is an adjective ending in "-y" having a literal meaning that it normally doesn't have. For example, in the clue "Sticky home?" (answered by NEST), "sticky" is jokingly taken to mean "made of sticks."

13-Down
When a very short answer is clued by a fill-in-the-blank in a title or quotation, chances are it's a multiword answer, often a two-letter word followed by "a." Even if the title is totally unfamiliar, a logical guess is often correct.

Puzzle 67

27-Across
To answer this clue, you don't need to know a thing about the city São Paulo.

24-Down
Here, try thinking of the first word as a noun rather than the adjective you'd normally expect.

Puzzle 68

45-Across
Although you might expect this clue to be answered by the name of another film, the answer instead is something that can "follow" either of these titles.

32-Down
For a clue that starts with "more than," think of an answer similar in meaning to the clue, but to a stronger degree.

Puzzle 69

59-Across
The reason this clue merits the question mark is because the second word must be interpreted in a way other than you'd expect—that is, it's neither a person nor a fictional character.

2-Down
In clues of this format, the item in quotes is something that the named person equated with the answer. Thus, the clue " 'A jealous mistress': Emerson" would be answered by ART, based on his quote "Art is a jealous mistress."

Puzzle 70

24-Across
"Comparatively" indicates a comparative adjective whose answer probably ends in -ER. Likewise, "Superlatively" yields a superlative adjective that very likely ends in -EST.

11-Down
This clue has a question mark not because it must be read in an unexpected way, but because it involves a fanciful pun (on the phrase "soul searching"). The answer is fairly straightforward.

Puzzle 71

38-Across
An unusually long and specific clue for something that doesn't sound familiar is usually a tip-off that, as you feared, you probably don't know the answer. (Or do you?) At least when you get the answer from the crossing words, you'll know exactly what it is.

56-Down
After solving enough crosswords, you'll realize that a "chemical suffix" is almost always ANE, ENE, IDE, or INE.

Puzzle 72

20-Across
A clue asking for a musical group with a three-letter name will almost always lead to REM, ELO, or TLC. These three names are easy to memorize, even if you know nothing about pop music.

29-Down
To answer this deceptive clue, you don't need to know a thing about the 1960s folk group Peter, Paul and Mary. Instead, be clever.

Puzzle 73

28-Across
Here is an example of a clue where a couple of vital missing pieces of information must be supplied by the solver. The "it" is not only a certain product, but a specific brand of it.

6-Down
Be careful not to miss the accent over the "é." That one little mark makes a big difference.

Puzzle 74

1-Across
If your crossing answers to 1-Across seem to give you an unlikely combination of letters, don't assume you've made a mistake. They are indeed odd. The constructor probably put his answer here precisely for its unusual looks.

22-Across
Often a clue naming a composer and a foreign-language song title, with a four-letter answer, yields ARIA. But not always!

Puzzle 75

7-Across
This clue requires a couple of mental leaps. For starters, note that the first word, "Ally," might be a proper name.

35-Across
Here is an example of a very advanced and quite difficult theme gimmick. Something must be added to all the capitalized clues throughout the puzzle before they make sense with their answers. This answer at 35-Across is a hint as to what . . . and where.

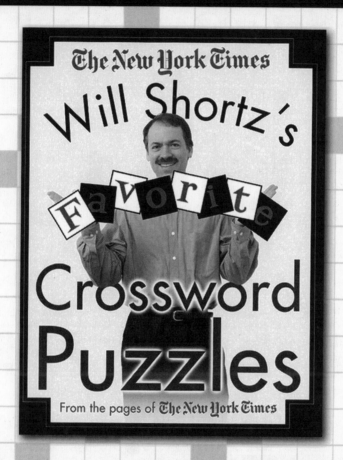

1

```
E G A D S   S A L S   S E P T
L O G I C   T A U T   T A R A
E A R T H Q U A K E   I T I S
C L O S E U P   E M B L E M S
        D O O R   E T N A
B E T A   D R I V E R S
A L I B I   P I N E   G A S
S A N A N D R E A S F A U L T
S L Y   C A I N   T H Y M E
    S U N B E L T   A S A P
  S L O B   D A H S
A M E R I C A   C O A C H E S
L I M B   A F T E R S H O C K
A L O E   B R E R   H A N O I
S E N T   S O N S   A N E N T
```

2

```
C H A W   S P U D   A D M E N
O A T H   A L T A   T R A L A
A R I A   F O A L   S I L L Y
L I T T L E W H I T E L I E S
      S E T S   H A L
J A U N T Y   P E R   S P U R
E L S E S   S A Y O K   O N E
W E E W I L L I E W I N K I E
E V A   N E A R S   D I E T S
L E S S   R V S   E N T R E E
      T O O   T R A P
I T S Y B I T S Y S P I D E R
W H A L E   R A S A   C A V E
A R L E S   I G O T   K N E E
S U E D E   B E N Z   S A N K
```

3

```
C H A P   G L A D   C H A N T
R O L E   H I R E   H O W I E
A B E T   O G L E   A T O N E
B O X E R S H O R T S   K E N
      O T T   U T T E R S
D A C H A S   A L T E R
E Q U A L   O M I T   A N K A
B U L L D O G E D I T I O N S
T A L L   U R N S   O N T O P
    O P T E D   O N S E T S
S T E W E D   A P E
L E X   P O O D L E S K I R T
E A T U P   S E A N   A G E E
P R O S E   L A M E   L O B E
T Y L E R   O D O R   E R A S
```

4

```
B E A M   S T A T   D R I B S
O R L Y   E E G S   R O G E T
P I E R   T A R P   E B O N Y
S E C R E T P A S S W O R D
      H A L O   T O T
S A M   G E T E V E N   S P A
K N I F E   L E E   A L A N
U N D E R C O V E R A G E N T
L I A R   H U E   S E E D S
L E S   H O T S P O T   P A Y
      A U K   A C R E
H I D D E N T R E A S U R E
L A D E D   O R A L   S C A R
A T O L L   R E D O   A L M A
M E L E E   M E E T   Y A P S
```

5

```
A M A S S   B R A G   I S M S
H A V O C   L I M O   S P I N
S W E A R   O P T S   O O N A
      P I T T E R P A T T E R
    P L U M E   A E R O S O L
C L I P P E T Y C L O P
O A F   S U M O   N E R D Y
P I E S   P I K E R   S E R A
S T R E P   E L I A   R O N
    D I N G D O N G D I N G
J U P I T E R   S A R G E
O N O M A T O P O E I A
N I L E   H O A R   N I M O Y
E T O N   E V I L   S N E R D
S Y S T   R E L Y   T S A R S
```

6

```
A L M S . H E S S E . O P A L
G O A T . A C M E S . P A L E
O G R E . B O O N S . E E L S
. B L A Z I N G S A D D L E S
G O B L E T . E Y E . L Y E .
T O O . D A M P . P H A S E .
O K R A . B O O . B O A . . .
. S O M E L I K E I T H O T .
. . I N E . E R R . A B E D .
A S H E N . R E D O . D E Y .
R A E . U P S . S A L U T E .
C H A R I O T S O F F I R E .
T A L E . P I A N O . C A R E
I R E S . P L U T O . I T E M
C A R T . A L L O T . T E D S
```

7

```
O S H A . S U L K . S C E N T
S P E W . A N O N . C O P E S
S U R F . D I C E . A L I C E
A R O U N D T H E C L O C K .
. . . L O L A . H E N . . . .
D A D . R E S C U E R . S T E
A D A P T . A T E . B A I T .
M O N T H A F T E R M O N T H
O R C A . S E E . A P T L Y .
N E E . S H E R M A N . E E L
. . S U E . I R I S . . . . .
. D A Y I N A N D D A Y O U T
B R U N T . R U D E . R O P E
T A N G O . A K I N . U Z I S
U T T E R . B E E T . P E N T
```

8

```
S H A D E . G E L T . P A P A
K A P U T . A M I E . I R O N
I N O N E . R A M S . N E W T
P A P E R C L I P S . K N E E
. . S N A I L . T S A R S .
W O K . A M C . B R E L . .
E D I B L E . F L E X I B L E
B O L A . L I B Y A . P I E R
B R O C C O L I . L O S T I T
. . K A T E . S T D . S S E .
T H E F T . A N O D E . . . .
R O L L . R A D A R B L I P S
A N T I . S L O P . A L C O A
C O O P . V E R A . L I O N S
E R N S . P E N T . L E N D S
```

9

```
A J A R . B L A C K . F O O T
L I L I . E E R I E . I N G E
E N D O F S T O R Y . N U L L
E X O . L O B O . W E A S E L
. . T O T E . B O L L . . .
H A B E A S . W O R K A D A Y
I N E R T . B A W D . N E B O
T E A M . F A S T S . S L O W
O M N I . A L T O . T W I R L
N O O N T I M E . C H E S T S
. . A I R Y . T I E R . . .
S C H L E P . P U T S . L E S
L O O M . L A S T R E S O R T
A L M A . A D I E U . U R G E
T E E N . Y E S E S . N E S T
```

10

```
A V I S . R I P E N . A C T S
M I L E . E R O D E . B L E U
P E L T . F O R G E . B O A R
. . H A U N T E D H O U S E .
C I A . I T S . L A T T E R .
U N M A D E . S T E M S . . .
B U M P E R C A R S . M A D .
B R A T . R I O . S A T E .
Y E N . T I L T A W H I R L
. . S N O B S . C R E D I T
O R P H A N . A C E . S P A .
M E R R Y G O R O U N D . . .
A G U E . U S E R S . O I L Y
H A N D . E L I T E . C I T E
A L E S . S O N A R . K I D S
```

11

R	A	D	I	I	■	Q	T	I	P	■	A	T	A	T
A	R	E	N	T	■	A	R	C	O	■	L	A	G	S
G	I	S	T	S	■	N	O	E	L	■	L	I	R	E
T	O	I	L	A	N	D	T	R	O	U	B	L	E	■
A	S	S	■	■	O	A	S	■	■	P	U	G	E	T
G	O	T	E	A	M	■	■	N	A	S	T	A	S	E
■	■	D	E	A	D	S	E	T	■	T	O	N		
L	A	B	O	R	D	A	Y	W	E	E	K	E	N	D
E	W	E	■	■	I	N	S	T	I	L	L	■	■	
S	A	D	S	A	C	K	■	■	N	O	M	A	A	M
T	Y	R	O	S	■	E	D	T	■	L	S	U		
■	W	O	R	K	I	N	P	R	O	G	R	E	S	S
B	E	L	T	■	S	O	S	O	■	M	I	X	E	S
U	G	L	I	■	I	R	O	N	■	A	L	I	N	E
N	O	S	E	■	S	A	M	E	■	T	E	S	T	S

12

M	I	D	A	S	■	L	A	D	S	■	L	A	M	B
A	R	E	N	A	■	O	P	E	C	■	A	V	E	R
L	A	N	D	L	U	B	B	E	R	■	B	I	T	E
T	N	T	■	O	R	E	■	R	U	N	O	V	E	R
■	■	L	O	G	■	D	E	F	E	R	■			
E	N	G	I	N	E	E	R	■	F	I	L	M	E	D
R	O	O	M	■	N	A	S	H	■	L	E	A	V	E
A	R	T	E	■	T	R	E	E	S	■	A	R	I	A
S	M	I	L	E	■	S	U	R	E	■	D	I	A	L
E	A	T	I	N	G	■	S	E	R	G	E	A	N	T
■	G	I	R	L	S	■	M	A	R	■				
R	U	S	H	D	I	E	■	P	O	L	■	O	F	F
E	T	A	T	■	L	A	T	I	N	L	O	V	E	R
S	A	G	E	■	L	R	O	N	■	O	P	E	R	A
T	H	A	R	■	S	N	A	G	■	N	A	N	N	Y

13

L	I	E	N	■	S	P	L	A	T	■	C	L	A	D
E	D	D	Y	■	C	L	O	V	E	■	A	O	N	E
E	I	S	E	N	H	O	W	E	R	■	U	L	N	A
Z	O	E	■	O	L	D	S	■	R	O	L	L	O	N
A	T	L	A	S	E	S	■	F	I	N	I	■		
■	P	I	P	■	T	R	E	E	F	E	R	N		
■	F	I	R	E	P	O	W	E	R	■	L	I	E	U
N	O	S	I	R	■	M	I	R	■	L	O	R	A	N
A	R	A	L	■	V	I	N	E	B	O	W	E	R	
B	A	Y	S	T	A	T	E	■	I	C	E	■		
■	H	A	M	S	■	T	O	U	R	I	S	T		
R	E	C	O	U	P	■	C	A	T	S	■	T	I	E
A	L	A	W	■	I	V	O	R	Y	T	O	W	E	R
M	I	N	E	■	R	E	M	O	P	■	R	A	G	S
P	E	E	R	■	E	L	A	T	E	■	I	S	E	E

14

G	L	O	B	■	A	J	A	R	■	A	E	S	O	P
R	O	U	E	■	L	U	L	U	■	G	R	A	P	E
I	N	S	E	V	E	N	T	H	H	E	A	V	E	N
P	E	T	R	I	■	G	O	R	E	■	T	O	R	A
■	■	S	T	E	■	A	M	O	R	A	L			
H	I	G	H	A	S	A	K	I	T	E	■			
O	D	I	E	■	P	S	A	T	■	A	G	R	E	E
M	E	L	B	A	■	P	R	S	■	T	O	A	D	S
E	A	T	A	T	■	I	O	N	S	■	I	V	E	S
■	O	N	C	L	O	U	D	N	I	N	E			
C	H	R	O	M	E	■	■	E	R	G	■			
R	E	A	R	■	M	A	S	T	■	A	D	A	G	E
O	N	T	O	P	O	F	T	H	E	W	O	R	L	D
S	C	O	N	E	■	R	E	E	D	■	W	E	A	N
S	E	N	O	R	■	O	W	E	S	■	N	A	D	A

15

F	I	N	A	L	■	C	A	L	M	■	P	U	B	S
A	R	E	N	A	■	A	R	E	A	■	A	S	A	P
N	E	W	T	S	■	M	I	N	X	■	R	A	T	A
■	S	I	T	U	P	S	T	R	A	I	G	H	T	
C	U	R	■	T	S	E	■	O	B	S	E	S	S	
O	N	E	D	G	E	■	H	A	S	■				
O	D	E	O	N	■	E	R	I	C	■	O	T	T	O
P	U	L	L	U	P	T	O	T	H	E	C	U	R	B
T	E	S	T	■	E	N	D	S	■	T	H	R	E	E
■	S	R	A	■	L	O	O	N	E	Y				
S	H	O	R	T	S	■	C	A	B	■	A	S	S	
P	U	S	H	U	P	D	A	I	S	I	E	S	■	
A	R	C	O	■	I	O	N	S	■	C	L	I	F	F
C	L	A	D	■	R	E	A	L	■	E	L	D	E	R
E	Y	R	E	■	E	R	L	E	■	S	E	E	D	Y

16

```
A F R O   N E A T   A S C O T
B L O B   A R L O   S O A P Y
C U B S C O U T S   T Y L E R
      C O M P O S E R   F R A
F A K E S I T   N O R M A N
O L I N   S P A S   O U S T
R O D E O S   A L I E N S
D E B   K I T B A G S   C P A
    R I S E R S   N O B L E S
S C O T   R A T S   L E A K
H I T T E R   P R I E S T S
A C H   W A R P L A N E
D E E R E   C H I C K P E A S
E R R O R   M I C E   E L I A
D O S E S   P L E D   D I L L
```

17

```
A M I D   R I F T S   E D G E
L I M O   O N E U P   W O R N
I N A N   M A N N A   E G A D
B I G S P E N D E R S   S N L
A M I   H O E S   S A T I E
B A N J O S   F A T C A T S
A L E U T   W A I L   T R E S
    M O N E Y B A G S
S T O P   O D E S   R U D E R
T Y C O O N S   C A P I T A
O P E N S   T E R I   L E I
N E A   H I G H R O L L E R S
E D N A   T E R R A   O M N I
R U I N   C R E E K   O M A N
S P C A   H E E D S   P A L S
```

18

```
S P R I G   F L I P   A L A S
A L A M O   I O T A   B O R E
D U M P S T R U C K   D O L E
E S P   S U M   H I T U P O N
    M I N E S   S E C
  T H E P A R E N T S T R A P
B O E R S   N E A T   A L I
R O L E   S P A W N   E D I T
A T L   S C O T   A R I E S
C H O O C H O O S T R A I N
    M A O   R H E T T
G A Z E B O S   A S I   A L E
A X E L   L U N C H S T R A Y
S I D E   E R I K   T W I N E
P S S T   D E N S   S O D A S
```

19

```
C A M P   R E D B U D   S P A
A G U A   E L A I N E   T A C
F I S T   F I R S T B L U S H
E L I T E   L O I   A P S E
S E C O N D H A N D   T I E D
    N C A A   S Y N O D
O S U   R N A   A Y E R S
R U N N I N G T H E B A S E S
E P C O T   T E X   T O T
    L O E S S   R E A P
R E A D   T H I R D W O R L D
E M I L   I O N   S T A I R
H O M E O F F I C E   A L V A
A T E   P L A T E R   S L I P
B E D   P E R S O N   H Y D E
```

20

```
C H E S S   G L O A T   A P E
P A S T E   R I F L E   F R A
A S S A I L A S A I L   F O R
      Z E S T   L O O S E
P E A N U T S   S T I R R E D
A L T E R S   T W I N E D
T I T L E   B R I N G   A S S
E T A L   L O U S Y   I F A T
R E C   P O O C H   A D O B E
    K A R A T E   P I E R R E
A C A D E M Y   P A R A D E D
M O T E L   H E L D
B R A   A F F I R M A F I R M
L A C   T O R S O   T I T A N
E L K   E X I S T   E R A T O
```

21

S	T	U	D		J	O	Y	S		D	W	A	R	F
H	O	N	E		A	R	E	A		R	O	D	E	O
O	T	I	S		S	L	A	M		E	V	A	D	E
W	A	T	C	H	M	Y	H	O	U	S	E			
	L	E	R	O	I		S	A	G	S		A	P	T
		Y	O	N	D		L	U	S	T	E	R		
R	A	M		F	E	E	D	M	Y	P	U	P	P	Y
O	L	E	G		W	E	E		M	A	S	T		
W	A	T	E	R	M	Y	L	A	W	N		R	I	O
A	M	E	L	I	A		D	E	A	L				
N	O	R		P	R	O	D		T	R	A	M	S	
		P	I	C	K	U	P	M	Y	M	A	I	L	
B	A	T	O	N		A	E	R	O		B	O	Z	O
E	X	A	L	T		P	L	O	P		D	R	E	W
G	E	C	K	O		I	S	M	S		A	I	D	E

22

A	C	T	S		S	K	E	W		D	I	S	C	O
D	R	O	P		T	O	R	I		E	V	I	A	N
H	O	L	Y	G	R	A	I	L		C	A	N	T	O
O	W	L		R	I	L	E	Y		A	N	G	E	R
C	D	S		I	D	A		I	D	O	L			
	B	L	E	S	S	E	D	E	V	E	N	T		
S	T	E	E	L		A	L	E	S		T	O	R	
H	E	L	D		L	A	Y	L	A		A	O	N	E
E	R	E		A	I	R	S		A	N	N	E	X	
D	I	V	I	N	E	C	O	M	E	D	Y			
	A	N	T	S		E	N	O		P	A	M		
M	A	T	T	E		U	N	S	E	R		I	C	Y
A	L	I	E	N		S	A	C	R	E	D	C	O	W
A	D	O	R	N		S	T	A	G		O	K	R	A
M	A	N	N	A		R	O	L	Y		N	Y	N	Y

23

L	I	P	S		I	R	M	A		L	O	S	E	S
A	C	H	E		T	O	A	D		U	S	U	R	P
S	H	I	M		C	O	M	O		L	A	N	A	I
	L	I	G	H	T	I	N	A	U	G	U	S	T	
S	C	O	N	E		E	I	S		E	P	E	E	
H	U	M	A	N	L	Y		S	A	G				
A	B	E	L		O	A	K		R	E	S	E	N	T
W	I	L	L	I	A	M	F	A	U	L	K	N	E	R
S	T	A	Y	E	D		C	U	L		E	D	G	E
		R	S	T		F	E	A	T	U	R	E		
B	A	S	E		U	R	I		S	C	R	O	D	
Y	O	K	N	A	P	A	T	A	W	P	H	A		
G	R	I	T	S		D	A	L	I		I	N	G	E
O	T	E	R	I		E	L	A	N		N	C	A	A
D	A	R	E	S		S	Y	N	E		G	E	L	T

24

S	A	R	A		N	E	A	T		W	A	L	L	S
P	L	O	P		O	N	M	E		A	V	O	I	D
A	L	M	S		I	D	E	A		S	I	N	A	I
S	W	E	E	T	S	U	R	R	E	N	D	E	R	
M	E	R		Y	E	R		D	A	T		S	L	O
S	T	O	O	P		E	A	R	S		C	O	I	L
		H	E	T		S	O	T		A	M	A	D	
	H	E	Y	B	I	G	S	P	E	N	D	E	R	
G	I	V	E		C	U	E		R	U	G			
A	L	E	S		K	I	S	S		D	E	A	N	S
M	A	N		D	E	N		N	A	G		D	E	C
	R	E	T	U	R	N	T	O	S	E	N	D	E	R
M	I	D	I	S		E	W	O	K		A	L	D	A
S	T	U	C	K		S	I	Z	E		D	E	E	P
G	Y	P	S	Y		S	T	E	W		A	D	D	S

25

S	P	O	T		A	L	O	H	A		C	A	M	P
A	I	D	A		M	A	N	E	S		O	V	E	R
G	E	O	R	G	E	B	U	S	H		M	I	N	I
E	R	R		A	L	E	S		G	I	L	D	S	
		R	O	I	L		S	A	R	C	A	S	M	
I	M	P	A	L	A		M	A	M	E				
C	O	O	N			S	O	L	I	T	A	I	R	E
E	L	E	C	T	I	O	N	A	N	A	G	R	A	M
D	E	T	H	R	O	N	E	D		N	O	T	I	
		A	W	A	Y		W	I	E	N	E	R		
F	L	A	T	C	A	R		S	I	C	S			
L	U	C	R	E		R	A	G	U		P	U	P	
A	S	T	I		H	E	B	U	G	S	G	O	R	E
S	T	E	P		A	L	I	C	E		U	S	S	R
H	Y	D	E		W	I	S	E	D		M	E	A	T

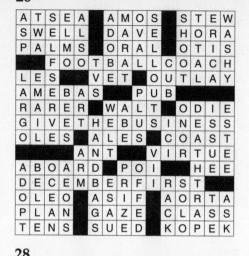
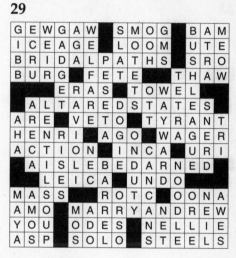

26

```
A T S E A   A M O S   S T E W
S W E L L   D A V E   H O R A
P A L M S   O R A L   O T I S
    F O O T B A L L C O A C H
L E S     V E T   O U T L A Y
A M E B A S     P U B
R A R E R   W A L T   O D I E
G I V E T H E B U S I N E S S
O L E S   A L E S   C O A S T
      A N T   V I R T U E
A B O A R D   P O I   H E E
D E C E M B E R F I R S T
O L E O   A S I F   A O R T A
P L A N   G A Z E   C L A S S
T E N S   S U E D   K O P E K
```

27

```
A B I G   A S T O   S P I C E
M A C E   D O O M   T A R O T
I S I T   D A T E   E L A T E
G I N G E R R O G E R S
A L G O R E   A D O   S U R
        A S T I   N I P P L E
A C C   S A G E A D V I C E
S O U T H   T A G   S T E E L
C U R R Y F A V O R   D R S
O L D A G E   E S A U
T D S   I D O   P L A T E S
      S E S A M E S T R E E T
E A T I N   S A L T   R A R E
A L I N E   I D E A   A S I A
R A C K S   S E A R   S E E K
```

28

```
J A M B   H A J J   I M A M S
O R A L   O M O O   N A T A L
T A X I   T A S K   Q U O T A
  B I T E S T H E B U L L E T
    Z E E   R O I   L Y E
A S P   L A P P   S R S
C H E W S T H E S C E N E R Y
T O N E   E P I   U L E E
S W A L L O W S T H E B A I T
    K I M   I Z O D   M D I
A V A   P I A   L E M
D I G E S T S T H E N E W S
I T A L Y   H E E D   Z E A L
O R I O N   E C R U   Z E R O
S O N I C   S H O P   O K A Y
```

29

```
G E W G A W   S M O G   B A M
I C E A G E   L O O M   U T E
B R I D A L P A T H S   S R O
B U R G   F E T E   T H A W
      E R A S   T O W E L
  A L T A R E D S T A T E S
A R E   V E T O   T Y R A N T
H E N R I   A G O   W A G E R
A C T I O N   I N C A   U R I
  A I S L E B E D A R N E D
    L E I C A   U N D O
M A S S   R O T C   O O N A
A M O   M A R R Y A N D R E W
Y O U   O D E S   N E L L I E
A S P   S O L O   S T E E L S
```

30

```
S L A M   A H E M   M E T R O
C I T E   D A T A   O R R I N
A M O S   O M N I   P R O S E
N E P A L P L A N E P A N E L
        A T E   V E T
L E A S T S T A L E T A L E S
E R N I E   M A R S   L A W
G I G S   T O O N S   M A G E
A C E   D O W N   A I M E D
L A R G E R E G A L G L A R E
      R P I   G E E
P A C E R C A P E R R E C A P
I R A T E   B O N N   C O L A
N I L E S   B O D E   H O O D
G A L L S   A L A R   O P U S
```

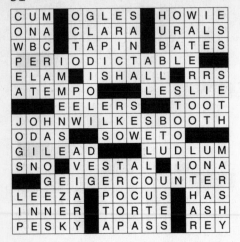

31

```
C U M   O G L E S   H O W I E
O N A   C L A R A   U R A L S
W B C   T A P I N   B A T E S
P E R I O D I C T A B L E
E L A M   I S H A L L   R R S
A T E M P O     L E S L I E
    E E L E R S     T O O T
J O H N W I L K E S B O O T H
O D A S     S O W E T O
G I L E A D   L U D L U M
S N O   V E S T A L   I O N A
  G E I G E R C O U N T E R
L E E Z A   P O C U S   H A S
I N N E R   T O R T E   A S H
P E S K Y   A P A S S   R E Y
```

32

```
C L O D   F A R A D   H E A L
P A V E   A P E R Y   A C L U
A X E L   K L E I N   S L I M
    R I T E O F P A S S A G E
S T R   A I M     S P L I N T
W R I G H T B R O T H E R S
A U D I O     H A Y
G E E S E   H I T   A C C R A
      S U N     F U R O R
  W R I T E H O M E A B O U T
C H A N E L   A L T   S T Y
R I G H T F I E L D E R S
A N T E   I S T L E   A B E T
T E A R   S A T E S   N O V A
E D G E   H Y A T T   G W E N
```

33

```
R I P E   D E E P S   R I F T
E M U S   A W A I T   I D E A
P U N T A M E T E R   G L A D
O S I E R S   E R E   H E R A
  C R I   U N R E S T
  P I S   B L U E P U N C I L
S O L   B E E P   P O O N A
T I L L A G E   B R E W P U B
E L I A S   S O A R   U S S
P U N M A N S H I P   O N E
  P L A T E S   O C H
I C E R   P A R   A L T A R S
O O Z E   A P P U N D A G E S
W I R Y   L L A M A   V E N T
A L A S   M E S A S   E N O S
```

34

```
S E E Y A   A L P O   J A B S
E R R O L   S O A K   O R E O
C R I M P   T A S S   U C L A
T S K   H A R D Y H A R H A R
      A V A   S O W
P C T   B O Y S T O W N U S A
L A W M E N   Y E T   O N T O
A P A R T   A R M   C O W E R
I R I S   A M I   F A K E I T
N A N C Y R E A G A N   D N A
    M T N   R I D
D R E W A S A L A R Y   M A O
R I T A   A M E S   B L U T O
I O U S   L E A P   A E S O P
Q T I P   E N D S   R A S P S
```

35

```
R O R E M   M O A B   R S V P
A D I E U   A R I A   E T A L
C O I N S U R E R S   F I L E
Y R S   T R I O   S A U C E D
      V A N E   M I N S K
M E T E R S   C O N T E S T S
A P H I D   R A N E E   W O N
N O E L   T A R O T   G I N O
I C H   G R I D S   P U T T O
C H I T L I N S   C A R H O P
  C R O C S   P E R U
O C C U P Y   B O O K   G E O
M O U E   C R O S S W O R D S
A M P S   L A O S   A N A I S
N A S T   E Y R E   Y E N T A
```

36

G	N	A	W	■	T	A	M	P	A	■	A	S	T	I
R	E	N	O	■	E	Q	U	I	P	■	S	P	O	T
A	U	T	O	■	R	U	L	E	R	■	S	A	Y	S
F	R	O	Z	E	N	A	C	C	O	U	N	T	S	■
T	A	N	Y	A	■	■	H	E	N	S	■	U	T	E
S	L	Y	■	R	A	F	■	■	S	A	I	L	O	R
■	■	D	N	A	L	A	B	■	■	B	A	R	A	■
■	F	R	E	S	H	A	S	A	D	A	I	S	Y	■
F	R	E	E	■	■	T	H	R	O	B	S	■	■	■
T	E	H	R	A	N	■	■	B	I	Z	■	J	O	S
S	S	E	■	Y	E	A	S	■	■	U	T	E	R	O
■	C	A	N	N	E	D	L	A	U	G	H	T	E	R
T	O	R	O	■	D	E	A	N	S	■	I	S	L	E
V	E	S	T	■	■	L	A	N	D	S	■	N	E	S	S
A	S	E	A	■	E	L	G	A	R	■	S	T	E	T

37

P	A	R	A	■	T	A	L	E	S	■	J	A	Z	Z
A	L	E	E	■	R	H	O	D	E	■	O	L	E	O
R	O	D	S	■	U	S	A	I	R	■	E	P	E	E
I	F	Y	O	U	D	O	N	T	P	A	Y	■	■	■
S	T	E	P	P	E	■	■	S	I	P	■	S	A	D
■	■	■	D	A	U	B	■	C	A	C	K	L	E	■
F	O	R	Y	O	U	R	E	X	O	R	C	I	S	M
A	B	I	E	■	■	G	E	M	■	■	C	R	A	M
W	I	L	L	T	H	E	R	E	S	U	L	T	B	E
N	E	L	L	I	E	■	S	N	U	G	■	■	■	■
S	S	S	■	R	A	H	■	■	R	H	O	N	D	A
■	■	R	E	P	O	S	S	E	S	S	I	O	N	■
S	H	E	A	■	S	A	H	I	B	■	C	E	N	T
K	I	E	V	■	O	R	A	T	E	■	A	C	N	E
I	S	L	E	■	N	Y	M	E	T	■	R	E	A	D

38

U	N	I	V	■	O	T	H	E	R	■	U	G	H
A	T	L	A	S	■	C	R	O	W	E	■	N	R	A
W	H	E	R	E	T	H	E	R	E	S	■	R	A	M
■	I	R	I	S	E	S	■	A	B	O	I	L	■
A	S	S	A	I	L	■	S	E	A	L	A	B	L	E
M	A	C	B	E	T	H	■	B	E	H	E	S	T	■
O	R	A	L	S	■	E	R	I	E	S	■	■	■
R	A	T	E	■	A	W	I	L	L	■	F	R	I	A
■	■	F	U	N	G	I	■	T	R	O	L	L	■
H	E	R	M	A	N	■	O	T	H	E	L	L	O
E	X	E	C	U	T	E	D	■	O	R	E	L	S	E
N	E	P	A	L	■	V	E	R	G	E	S	■	■
R	D	A	■	T	H	E	R	E	S	A	P	L	A	Y
Y	R	S	■	E	R	R	E	D	■	D	I	A	N	E
V	A	T	■	D	E	S	K	S	■	N	I	N	A

39

A	L	P	S	■	S	P	I	N	S	■	T	R	A	M
S	O	R	E	■	O	R	N	O	T	■	I	A	G	O
A	T	O	M	■	L	O	D	G	E	■	E	B	R	O
■	F	I	V	E	P	O	S	T	E	R	B	E	D	■
S	K	A	■	E	R	E	■	■	C	R	I	E	S	■
N	I	N	E	G	A	L	L	O	N	H	A	T	■	■
A	R	E	N	A	■	■	I	D	E	O	■	■
G	I	R	D	■	C	U	B	E	D	■	P	E	N	N
■	■	E	A	S	Y	■	C	O	P	A	Y	■
■	S	I	X	D	E	A	D	L	Y	S	I	N	S
B	L	I	N	I	■	■	E	O	S	■	P	O	E
E	I	G	H	T	Y	E	A	R	I	T	C	H	■
B	A	N	E	■	A	D	M	I	T	■	R	A	T	A
O	N	E	R	■	L	E	A	V	E	■	A	N	O	N
P	A	T	E	■	E	N	T	E	R	■	B	Y	E	S

40

N	A	B	S	■	B	A	N	■	H	E	E	H	A	W
O	R	E	O	■	U	T	E	■	A	L	B	I	N	O
T	E	A	L	■	G	O	V	■	S	T	A	N	C	E
B	O	N	D	J	A	M	E	S	B	O	N	D	■
A	L	E	■	A	B	S	■	U	R	N	■	U	F	O
D	A	D	D	Y	O	■	M	N	O	■	B	I	L	E
■	■	E	V	O	K	E	S	■	W	I	S	E	R
■	H	O	M	E	S	W	E	E	T	H	O	M	E	■
D	A	F	O	E	■	A	T	T	H	A	T	■
A	R	F	S	■	R	N	S	■	E	L	A	P	S	E
Y	E	S	■	S	E	Z	■	A	B	E	■	R	E	X
■	T	I	M	E	A	F	T	E	R	T	I	M	E	■
B	L	A	R	E	S	■	L	E	A	■	O	M	I	T
R	E	G	A	L	E	■	O	U	R	■	M	E	T	E
A	G	E	N	T	S	■	P	P	S	■	B	R	E	R

41

```
GALA . LASER . SHAQ
IBET . ULTRA . MENU
GETTYSBURG . AIDE
ISOLATED . GORDIE
. . ELSE . FIFTEEN
UPSET . . LENTIL .
ROT . ASKING . EBBS
GORE . CISCO . SERA
ELAN . ATTEND . RIP
. STILTS . WAGES
SOBERLY . BEES .
PRONTO . SIDESTEP
LOUT . PITTSBURGH
INRE . ERASE . ROAD
TOGS . DARYL . ENDS
```

42

```
VIN¢ . BEAU . ¢AURS
ESAU . EXIT . RIPEN
STIR . DADA . ASPIE
TORYISM . HELLENE
SOAPDISH . OPERAS
. . LAD . EDNA .
ROTA . ECRU . RACES
FRANZ . AOL . KRAFT
DENTE . SILT . EDGY
. . ROTC . HOY .
BASSOS . SCROOGES
ELLIPSE . REPULSE
GLADE . IDEA . DOTE
EATER . REED . EVER
THES¢ . ENDS . ¢ERS
```

43

```
GREG . CLAWS . TECS
RARA . RELIC . OSLO
ADAM . OUTDO . STUN
MATERS . HERESIES
PROFESSORPLUM .
. . IDEA . IMPART
HUSSY . TITO . TOO
INTHEDININGROOM
CDR . INST . LARKS
KOALAS . HOAR .
. WITHTHEWRENCH
APPLEPIE . NEBULA
MOOT . ABASE . IBIS
OGLE . NEVER . TINT
SOLD . STYES . SAGE
```

44

```
BANG . OMEN . EATON
UPON . PUMA . TERRY
METACOMET . CRIES
PREWAR . REDEAGLE
. . STAY . OTT .
ALCOHOL . OSCEOLA
DIODE . ALPE . CON
DELAWAREPROPHET
UTO . LIDO . NURSE
PONTIAC . SADNESS
. . RAN . NENE .
TECUMSEH . ACTNOW
APIAN . BLACKHAWK
PIANO . RENI . USER
SCOTT . ORAN . GASP
```

45

```
BAOBAB . PAW . RUB
MANANA . IMRE . INE
WHACKSPAPER . VWS
. KLEIN . CICERO
ABASE . SOCK . ERAT
SOB . RASPS . TSPS
THROWIN . ARRET .
IRONIC . EERIER
. NENES . DEFACTO
ETCH . CHORD . KAT
SISI . HERA . LISTS
SETTEE . SCOOT .
EPA . SCHOOLTACKS
NIL . SKIN . ATLAST
ENE . SDS . FOLDUP
```

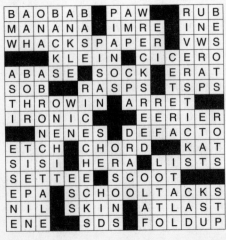

46

```
A P P L E S   V A N I S H E S
S H E I L A   A D O R A B L E
W I N S O M E L O S E S O M E
A L O T   B E L   E S E
N I L   G O L E M     S I N G
  P O S E     J A M B   N E A
  G O O D C O P B A D C O P
S K I D D O O   L A T R I N E
H E S A I D S H E S A I D
A N T   C O T E   A P E D
G O S H     S C O R N   N A M
  O R B   T O E   E T N A
O N A G A I N O F F A G A I N
P O M A N D E R   E A G L E S
T R I N K E T S   R A S S L E
```

47

```
C U L P   T A B   M I L T O N
O R A L   A T O   A R I O S O
M A M A S B O Y   R E P L A N
B L A C K A N D     L I L Y
    E I R E   B R E D
J A M M E D   D R E S S I N
O C T A D   B E E F S   M E L
S T A T   H A L A S   T E R I
H U P   C U R E D   C R A V E
  P O P L A R S   C R O N E S
    R A C Y   P R E P
  H E A T     E L E P H A N T
R E M I T S   C O N T I N U E
A R I S E N   O W N   E T N A
T O R E R O   N S A   S I N K
```

48

```
A B B A S   T R O N   A R T Y
S W A L E   S E R B   R O A M
S A I L S T H E C C C C C C C
A N T   T A I L   H A S T A
M A S S E U R   S O U R
    T T T T T G R O U P S
B O G U S     H A L L   G A L
O M E N   C H O R E   A L L A
I N E   S O A R   B L I M P
L I K E P P I N A P O D
  D R A G   D A D A I S M
S C H W A     M O D E   N A E
T H E Y Y Y M E N S G I F T S
E A R N   A N T I   A C E I N
W R E N   M O S S   S I R E E
```

49

```
S T A T   O L D S   U N S E T
A R M Y   N E R O   N O L T E
W I M P   C O U P   S C O N E
  G O E S R I G H T A H E A D
    A L E X   O F A
S I N B A D   C A M E N E A R
E M U   V I S O R   C L I O
W A L K S T W O A B R E A S T
O G L E   A L L A H   T L C
N O S E J O B S   R U P E E S
    P E R   A C M E
G E T S T A K E N A B A C K
O D E T S   O M A R   P O N D
A G R E E   O M I T   O V E R
T E M P T   L A S S   D E W Y
```

50

```
E M I L Y P O S T   I R I S H
G A M E T A B L E   T E N T O
G R A N D S L A M   A S S E S
A G C Y   T A I   S L E E V E
R E S A L E   N O H I T T E R
    A R C   P A C T
H O L E I N O N E   L I N T
A D U L T   P E N   A E T N A
H A M M   T O U C H D O W N
  S O L I   P A M
H A T T R I C K   S E A H A G
I M A R E T   Y A H   D O M E
P I X E L   D O U B L E R U N
P L I E S   I T S A B L A S T
O E S T E   P O T R O A S T S
```

51

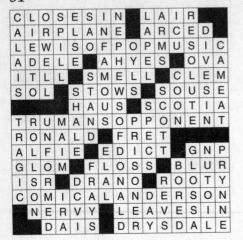

```
C L O S E S I N ▪ L A I R ▪ ▪
A I R P L A N E ▪ A R C E D ▪
L E W I S O F P O P M U S I C
A D E L E ▪ A H Y E S ▪ O V A
I T L L ▪ S M E L L ▪ C L E M
S O L ▪ S T O W S ▪ S O U S E
▪ ▪ H A U S ▪ S C O T I A ▪
T R U M A N S O P P O N E N T
R O N A L D ▪ F R E T ▪ ▪ ▪
A L F I E ▪ E D I C T ▪ G N P
G L O M ▪ F L O S S ▪ B L U R
I S R ▪ D R A N O ▪ R O O T Y
C O M I C A L A N D E R S O N
▪ N E R V Y ▪ L E A V E S I N
▪ ▪ D A I S ▪ D R Y S D A L E
```

52

```
N E S T S ▪ P A S T ▪ S H U N
A L E R T ▪ O S L O ▪ P O P E
T A L I A ▪ S T I N G I E S T
L L A F P O S I T I O N ▪ ▪
▪ ▪ O L D E R ▪ ▪ D A C H A
P I L L E D ▪ C R O C H E T
A M I D ▪ P M U H W H A L E
P A N ▪ A I L E R O N ▪ L E S
Y G G I P R I D E ▪ C E N T
R E U N I T E ▪ E M O T E S
I S A A C ▪ B O S U N ▪ ▪
▪ R E T R A U Q S N E A K
J U D A S K I S S ▪ C O L I N
F R O G ▪ O M I T ▪ A T A R I
K N E E ▪ S E E S ▪ T E N E T
```

53

```
S L O W ▪ R O S H ▪ A R T E
A E R I E ▪ A S T O ▪ L E I A
S A N T A ▪ J K R O W L I N G
E N A C T S ▪ A U D I ▪ N H L
B O T H ▪ O A R M E N ▪ D O E
O N E C E N T ▪ D O T E R S
▪ ▪ R E A T A ▪ ▪ E E N
▪ H A R R Y P O T T E R ▪ ▪
▪ R E F ▪ ▪ T R A I N ▪ ▪
B E A T A T ▪ S P E W E R S
A N D ▪ C R U S O E ▪ I N O N
S A L ▪ I O N A ▪ D A Z Z L E
Q U I D D I T C H ▪ G A Y L E
U L N A ▪ K I R I ▪ A R M O R
E T E S ▪ A L E S ▪ D E N S
```

54

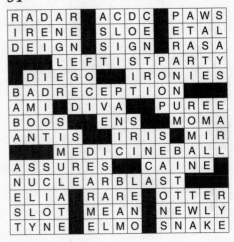

```
R A D A R ▪ A C D C ▪ P A W S
I R E N E ▪ S L O E ▪ E T A L
D E I G N ▪ S I G N ▪ R A S A
▪ ▪ L E F T I S T P A R T Y
▪ D I E G O ▪ ▪ I R O N I E S
B A D R E C E P T I O N ▪ ▪
A M I ▪ D I V A ▪ P U R E E
B O O S ▪ E N S ▪ M O M A
A N T I S ▪ I R I S ▪ M I R
▪ ▪ M E D I C I N E B A L L
A S S U R E S ▪ C A I N E
N U C L E A R B L A S T ▪ ▪
E L I A ▪ R A R E ▪ O T T E R
S L O T ▪ M E A N ▪ N E W L Y
T Y N E ▪ E L M O ▪ S N A K E
```

55

```
I S A S ▪ A H E M ▪ G A N E F
R U N T ▪ T O R A ▪ O L O R D
A L T A ▪ R O L L E D O V E R
Q U I R K O F E I G H T ▪ ▪
▪ ▪ D L I I ▪ ▪ G O O G O O
▪ Q U E S T I O N O F A C T
M E U S E ▪ ▪ G O O D ▪ N A T
A N A T ▪ F L I N G ▪ O G L E
M I I ▪ O L A V ▪ B L E A R
M A N O F E W E W O R D S ▪
A C T I V E ▪ ▪ I D I G ▪ ▪
▪ ▪ L A C K O F E E L I N G
R A K E L E A V E S ▪ O L E O
O T A R U ▪ M E L S ▪ R I C E
T E N S E ▪ A N Y A ▪ Y A K S
```

56

I	N	A	N	E		A	P	O	P		B	I	K	E
N	O	N	E	T		S	I	M	I		O	R	E	L
A	T	T	I	C		S	T	I	N	G	R	A	Y	S
W	E	I	G	H	S	T	A	T	I	O	N			
E	S	C	H	E	W			S	O	N	A	T	A	S
			D	E	E	P		N	E	G	A	T	E	
	T	V	S		A	C	E	S		B	A	S	R	A
T	H	A	T	S	T	H	E	W	A	Y	I	T	I	S
A	R	G	O	T		O	V	A	L		N	E	A	
R	E	U	N	E	D		E	M	I	L				
S	W	E	E	P	E	A		G	A	S	S	E	D	
			C	U	R	D	S	A	N	D	W	H	E	Y
A	U	T	O	P	I	L	O	T		L	E	A	R	N
O	P	A	L		D	I	D	O		E	D	D	I	E
K	I	N	D		E	B	A	N		R	E	Y	E	S

57

P	A	T	T	I		A	S	I	A		G	I	A	N
O	C	H	O	S		B	I	C	S		E	D	G	Y
S	T	A	Y	O	F	E	X	E	C	U	T	I	O	N
T	H	I	S	L	I	T	T	L	E	P	I	G	G	Y
			T	A	R	S	I		T	O	T			
C	O	Y	O	T	E		M	A	I	N		C	U	R
A	Z	U	R	E		M	E	R	C		C	O	L	E
S	A	L	E	S	R	E	S	I	S	T	A	N	C	E
E	W	E	S		A	L	F	A		U	R	G	E	D
D	A	S		M	I	D	I		D	R	E	A	R	Y
			S	O	N		F	R	O	N	T			
I	C	A	N	N	O	T	T	E	L	L	A	L	I	E
P	L	E	A	S	U	R	E	S	E	E	K	I	N	G
S	U	R	F		T	I	E	A		F	E	R	R	O
A	B	O	U		S	O	N	Y		T	R	E	E	S

58

P	I	R	A	T	E	S	H	I	P		R	E	I	D
O	N	E	T	O	O	M	A	N	Y		A	N	N	A
R	E	C	O	N	S	I	D	E	R		S	L	I	M
C	R	O	W	E		L	A	D	E		P	A	T	S
I	T	I	N		R	E	G	I	S		B	R	I	E
N	I	L		C	A	R	O	B		L	E	G	A	L
E	A	S	T	E	R			L	A	U	R	E	L	
			A	R	E	A		E	N	G	R			
	A	S	T	E	R	N		K	E	Y	P	A	D	
A	N	T	E	S		T	E	C	H	S		A	C	E
S	T	A	R		T	I	N	A	S		P	R	E	P
S	E	N	T		A	G	A	R		L	A	T	T	E
I	N	D	O		C	O	M	M	I	S	S	I	O	N
S	N	I	T			I	N	E	E	D	A	H	A	N	D
T	A	N	S		T	E	L	L	S	T	A	L	E	S

59

D	E	V	E	L	O	P	M	E	N	T	A	R	E	A
E	D	I	T	O	R	I	A	L	C	O	L	U	M	N
S	I	D	E	W	A	L	K	A	R	T	I	S	T	S
C	E	E	S		T	O	E	S			S	E	S	E
				B	E	T	A		D	S	T			
	F	O	A	M		C	O	O	T		M	O	M	
L	O	S	T	O	P	P	O	R	T	U	N	I	T	Y
A	C	T	I	V	E	I	N	T	E	R	E	S	T	S
W	A	I	T	I	N	G	F	O	R	G	O	D	O	T
S	L	A		E	A	S	E			E	N	O	S	
		I	S	L		S	A	S	S					
S	C	A	N		E	S	P	Y		G	A	G	A	
C	O	N	C	E	S	S	I	O	N	A	I	R	E	S
A	R	T	U	R	O	T	O	S	C	A	N	I	N	I
R	A	I	S	E	S	O	N	E	S	H	O	P	E	S

60

C	O	Q		F	L	O	R	A		O	P	C	I	T
O	N	A		L	I	E	I	N		N	U	I	T	S
M	E	N	D	E	L	I	A	N		A	L	O	O	P
M	A	D	E	M	I	L	L	I	O	N	S			
	D	A	L	I				E	D	A	M	E	S	
	I	S	W	A	R		D	O	T	E	L	L		
G	A	O		H	I	S	E	M	I	N	E	N	C	E
A	L	B	A		Z	I	P	U	P		S	L	I	D
B	I	O	C	H	E	M	I	C	A	L		O	D	S
O	N	E	T	O	N		N	H	L	E	R			
N	E	S	T	L	E				G	O	A	T		
			H	I	D	D	E	N	H	A	L	V	E	S
O	H	A	R	E		E	X	C	E	L	L	E	N	T
J	U	D	E	S		B	E	A	L	L		R	K	O
O	N	S	E	T		S	C	A	L	Y		S	S	W

61

```
G A F F . B A R B E R S H O P
R A I L . O B O E D A M O R E
E R N O . W E L L S P O K E N
E G G . P E L E . E G E S T .
T H E F E D . . P O E . . . .
. . R O E . I S U P . D I S C
R O B E R T O C L E M E N T E
E M O T I O N A L R E S C U E
N O W I N S I T U A T I O N S
T O L D . C U S P . E R N . .
. . . L A M . T O E T A P .
R E E D Y . W H I R . E K E
E X T I N C T I O N . A M I R
P I N E N E E D L E . U P T O
S T A T E T R E E S . S T A N
```

62

```
A S I S . S H E I K . G A V E
R O M P . L A R V A . O L I N
C B E R . A R N A Z . B L O C
H E L E A V E S N O . S O L O
E I D E R . . S O P . C A R .
S T A . M Y R A . S E D A T E
. . A R O U S E . T O T E S
. T O N E U N S T E R N E D .
V E I N S . S E A D O G . . .
I M L A T E . S T A C . S A T
O P S . S D I . . K A T I E
L O T S . I S A A C S T E R N
I R O N . S O U S A . A V I S
N A N O . O L D E R . L I N E
S L E W . N A I A D . L E G S
```

63

```
S D I . A K E L A . A T S E A
A R M . D O L E S . L U C A S
D E A R J O H N L E T T E R S
S A G E . K I D A R O U N D .
A M I D . . I N N S . E R G .
C O N F I D A N T E . T R U E
K N E L L I N G . T H Y M E
. . . A L D A . R O H E .
G A N G S . P O T R O A S T
E G O S . A M E N C O R N E R
R E F . A D A R . I N R E
. S A C R E D C O W . S U P S
P A U L I N E E P I S T L E S
O G L E S . O P A R T . U N E
G O T M E . F T L E E . S T S
```

64

```
. N E S T L E . B E A M E R S
C O A C H E D . R A D I O E R
A S S U R E D . A R I A N N A
L O T T O J A C K P O T . . .
M A E . . S H E . S A B L E
S P R A W L . I S H . N I P
. . W H A T S H I S N A M E
E C O N O M Y . O P A L I N E
M O M S A P P L E P I E . .
U M A . S E E . O N R A M P
S O N A R . W V A . . B I O
. . . T O U R I S T C L A S S
M I N I S K I . P A L A T E S
O N A D I E T . I R O N O R E
E D M E E S E . C O D E R S .
```

65

```
B A C K S L A P S . E R R O R
I R O N H O R S E . L O I R E
S C R E A M S A T . F A B L E
T H I E V E . T A L I S M A N
R A N . E I N . I N T E N T
O I N K . N E A T O . A D E
S C E N E . U L A N B A T O R
. . . I N T R A N S I T . .
W H I T E R O C K . L I L A C
H E N . I N K E D . T A R O
E N C A S E . D E B . Y O M
E R I C I D L E . P O P S U P
L Y S I S . A P P A L O O S A
E V E N S . S P O R T S F A N
R I D G Y . T S E T S E F L Y
```

66

```
S S H A P E D   W A S S A I L
C H O L E R A   I M P A S S E
O U T D R A W   T I L T S A T
O N E A C T     C D I I I
P T L   H O U G H   T E S L A
    R T E   N O E L   T A N
C R E A S E R E S I S T A N T
L O S T O N E S B A L A N C E
I S T A N D C O R R E C T E D
C I A   S L U E   D O E
K N U T E   A T W A R   D A B
    R A D I I   S I M I L E
R E A L I S M   U P D A T E S
P A N I C L E   P E E K O U T
M U T A T E D   I N S E R T S
```

67

```
I M A R E T   T H E L W O R D
N O M A Y O   R E F E R R E R
A N N L E E   A L L E Y W A Y
S A I L S   S N E A K   E P I
T R O Y   H A S N T   E L E C
A C T   M A R I A   T I L D E
T H I S I S I T   A U G
E S C O R T S   O N T H E Q T
    W E E   M I N O T A U R
P O M E S   D I N E R   R O I
A C A D   D E S K S   A T T N
C T S   G U E S S   C R O A K
K A T M A N D U   P H O E B E
O V E R S E E S   B A S A L T
N O R T H S E A   S T E R E S
```

68

```
B R U S H E D U P   M A C A W
R U P P A R E N A   A D O B E
A N T I G E N I C   T E N O N
I T O N   S T E R E   T U T
D O N A L D   S O Y   O T T
    L I E A B E D S   U F O
L A S T M I N U T E   G R A B
U N C A P   T N T   P I E C E
S N A P   L I K E M I N D E D
T E M   L A B O R I N G
A M P   I I I   A G E I S M
F E E   E C O L I   R O P E
T A R T S   T U R N S A W A Y
E R E C T   I N O C U L A T E
R A D I O   C A N O P E N E R
```

69

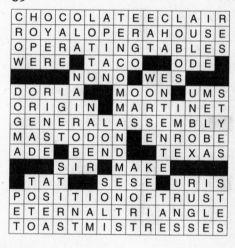

```
C H O C O L A T E E C L A I R
R O Y A L O P E R A H O U S E
O P E R A T I N G T A B L E S
W E R E   T A C O   O D E
        N O N O   W E S
D O R I A   M O O N   U M S
O R I G I N   M A R T I N E T
G E N E R A L A S S E M B L Y
M A S T O D O N   E N R O B E
A D E   B E N D   T E X A S
      S I R   M A K E
  T A T   S E S E   U R I S
P O S I T I O N O F T R U S T
E T E R N A L T R I A N G L E
T O A S T M I S T R E S S E S
```

70

```
S P A R T A     B R E A S T
E L D E R S   P A U L I N E
A E O L U S   C A S T I R O N
M A R A C A   A V I S   M R I
  S E X K I T T E N   B A K E
      S L A T S   W R I E R
    L I T A N Y   C H I L L S
    S A R O N G   S L I D E S
A C C E P T   F L U T E D
T H E N S   G L O B E
W E R E   D E A T H W I S H
A D A   B E A K   O I N K E D
T U T E L A R Y   U N L A C E
E L E V E N S   S E E T H E
R E S E D A     E S T E E M
```

71

B	E	E	F	J	E	R	K	Y	■	S	E	C	T	S
A	L	L	O	R	N	O	N	E	■	H	E	A	R	T
F	L	I	P	S	I	D	E	S	■	E	E	R	I	E
F	E	D	S	■	D	E	E	M	E	D	■	D	U	E
I	R	E	■	O	L	A	N	■	R	C	M	P		
N	Y	S	E	■	S	U	S	A	N	■	E	A	V	E
■	T	A	C	T	■	M	O	V	E	S	I	N		
A	R	G	U	E	R	■	B	I	K	E	R	S		
B	A	L	D	R	I	C	■	E	L	M	O	■		
S	T	Y	E	■	P	H	O	N	E	■	F	U	D	D
T	I	C	S	■	P	E	P	S	■	G	R	E		
R	O	E	■	O	S	M	I	U	M	■	D	A	I	S
U	N	R	I	P	■	I	N	R	E	S	E	R	V	E
S	A	O	N	E	■	S	E	E	S	A	F	T	E	R
E	L	L	E	N	■	E	S	S	A	Y	T	E	S	T

72

S	T	E	P	S	A	S	I	D	E	■	I	D	E	S
P	A	P	E	R	M	O	N	E	Y	■	N	E	X	T
A	M	E	L	I	O	R	A	T	E	■	C	A	T	O
C	A	R	T	■	R	E	M	■	C	O	O	L	I	O
E	R	G	■	R	E	C	O	R	D	I	N	G		
R	A	N	O	F	F	■	S	E	N	T	E	N	C	E
S	C	E	N	E	I	■	S	I	T	■	G	T	S	
■	T	E	R	I	■	L	A	M	B	■				
T	E	R	■	S	D	I	■	C	O	M	S	A	T	
O	N	E	T	O	T	E	N	■	T	O	W	H	E	E
S	T	A	R	K	N	E	S	S	■	O	R	R		
T	E	R	E	S	A	■	U	P	S	■	F	R	A	S
A	R	E	A	■	M	A	R	I	O	N	E	T	T	E
D	I	N	T	■	E	T	E	R	N	I	T	I	E	S
A	N	D	Y	■	S	C	R	E	E	N	T	E	S	T

73

M	A	L	T	S	H	O	P	■	R	A	F	F	L	E
A	R	E	A	C	O	D	E	■	A	L	L	I	E	S
I	C	E	W	A	T	E	R	■	S	E	A	N	C	E
L	A	W	■	M	E	S	S	J	A	C	K	E	T	■
E	D	A	M	■	S	O	O	■	S	E	T	U	P	
D	E	Y	S	■	S	A	N	K	A	■	S	U	R	E
■	G	O	T	■	A	E	R	O	■	N	E	W		
■	S	I	T	D	O	W	N	D	I	N	N	E	R	■
A	T	M	■	S	O	H	O	■	S	A	O			
N	A	P	A	■	D	E	N	S	E	■	I	B	I	S
C	L	O	M	P	■	A	G	E	■	R	E	N	E	
■	B	L	U	E	S	T	R	E	A	K	■	N	A	N
B	A	I	L	E	Y	■	A	R	S	O	N	I	S	T
I	N	T	E	R	N	■	T	E	E	N	A	G	E	R
T	S	E	T	S	E	■	A	D	A	G	E	N	C	Y

74

A	M	F	M	R	A	D	I	O	■	F	A	N	S	
B	E	L	I	E	V	I	N	G	■	A	L	I	E	N
R	A	I	N	M	A	K	E	R	■	P	E	R	M	A
O	N	T	H	E	■	R	E	V	I	E	W	E	R	
A	S	T	■	D	U	E	T	■	E	N	C	A	S	E
D	I	E	■	I	N	D	I	A	N	G	I	V	E	R
■	T	R	I	A	L	D	A	T	E	■	E	E	S	
■	M	L	I	I	■	H	E	M	S	■				
■	A	P	P	■	V	E	N	E	R	A	T	E	D	
C	L	A	I	R	E	D	A	N	E	S	■	R	A	S
L	I	N	E	A	L	■	T	A	D	S	■	A	R	T
A	M	E	T	H	Y	S	T	■	A	I	S	L	E	
C	E	L	I	A	■	A	I	R	S	C	R	E	E	N
K	N	E	E	L	■	P	E	T	E	R	A	R	N	O
S	T	D	S	■	P	R	E	T	E	N	S	E	S	

75

T	H	A	T	I	S	■	C	A	L	I	S	T	A
H	O	M	E	L	Y	■	O	R	I	E	N	T	A	L
E	N	A	M	E	L	■	D	O	M	I	N	A	N	T
H	O	R	A	■	T	O	W	S	■	O	T	T	O	
A	R	I	S	E	■	O	R	E	■	C	U	E	S	
G	I	L	■	S	A	W	■	R	U	P	E	E	S	
U	N	L	■	T	R	I	O	■	N	O	N			
E	G	O	C	E	N	T	R	I	C	I	T	I	E	S
■	O	R	I	■	K	O	L	N	■	N	A	P		
■	C	L	O	S	E	T	■	W	E	T	■	C	T	A
R	A	I	L	■	O	V	A	■	E	T	H	E	R	
I	M	A	N	■	E	R	I	N	■	A	A	R	E	
V	E	N	E	R	A	T	E	■	D	E	B	R	I	S
E	R	A	S	U	R	E	S	■	A	P	O	G	E	E
T	A	S	S	E	L	S	■	D	I	R	E	S	T	

The New York Times

Crossword Puzzles

The #1 name in crosswords

**Millions of fans know that *New York Times* crosswords
are the pinnacle of puzzledom.
Challenge your brain with these quality titles from St. Martin's Griffin.**

Available at your local bookstore or online at **nytimes.com/nytstore**

Coming Soon

Easy Omnibus Vol. 2	0-312-32035-3	$11.95/$17.95 Can.
Daily Omnibus Vol. 13	0-312-32031-0	$11.95/$17.95 Can.
Sunday Crosswords Vol. 29	0-312-32038-8	$9.95/$14.95 Can.
Daily Crosswords Vol. 65	0-312-32034-5	$9.95/$14.95 Can.
Large-Print Crosswords to Boost Your Brainpower	0-312-32037-X	$11.95/$17.95 Can.
Large-Print Crossword Omnibus Vol. 5	0-312-32036-1	$12.95/$18.95 Can.
Crosswords for Your Bedside	0-312-32032-9	$6.95/$9.95 Can.

Special Editions

Ultimate Omnibus	0-312-31622-4	$17.95/$25.95 Can.
Crossword All-Stars	0-312-31004-8	$9.95/$14.95 Can.
Will Shortz's Favorites	0-312-30613-X	$9.95/$14.95 Can.
Bonus Crosswords	0-312-31003-X	$9.95/$14.95 Can.

Daily Crosswords

Monday through Friday	0-312-30058-1	$9.95/$14.95 Can.
Daily Crosswords Vol. 64	0-312-31458-2	$9.95/$14.95 Can.
Daily Crosswords Vol. 63	0-312-30947-3	$9.95/$14.95 Can.
Daily Crosswords Vol. 62	0-312-30512-5	$9.95/$14.95 Can.
Daily Crosswords Vol. 61	0-312-30057-3	$9.95/$14.95 Can.
Daily Crosswords Vol. 60	0-312-28799-2	$9.95/$14.95 Can.
Daily Crosswords Vol. 59	0-312-28413-6	$9.95/$14.95 Can.

Easy Crosswords

Easy Crosswords Vol. 4	0-312-30448-X	$9.95/$14.95 Can.
Easy Crosswords Vol. 3	0-312-28912-X	$9.95/$14.95 Can.
Easy Crosswords Vol. 2	0-312-28172-2	$9.95/$14.95 Can.

Tough Crosswords

Tough Crosswords Vol. 11	0-312-31455-6	$10.95/$15.95 Can.
Tough Crosswords Vol. 10	0-312-30060-3	$10.95/$15.95 Can.
Tough Crosswords Vol. 9	0-312-28173-0	$10.95/$15.95 Can.

Sunday Crosswords

Sunday Crosswords Vol. 28	0-312-30515-X	$9.95/$14.95 Can.
Sunday Crosswords Vol. 27	0-312-28414-4	$9.95/$14.95 Can.

Large Print Crosswords

Large-Print Daily	0-312-31457-4	$10.95/$15.95 Can.
Large-Print Crossword Omnibus Vol. 4	0-312-30514-1	$12.95/$18.95 Can.
Large-Print Crossword Omnibus Vol. 3	0-312-28441-1	$12.95/$18.95 Can.

Omnibus

Easy Omnibus Vol. 1	0-312-30513-3	$11.95/$17.95 Can.
Daily Omnibus Vol. 12	0-312-30511-7	$11.95/$17.95 Can.
Daily Omnibus Vol. 11	0-312-28412-8	$11.95/$17.95 Can.
Sunday Omnibus Vol. 7	0-312-30950-3	$11.95/$17.95 Can.
Sunday Omnibus Vol. 6	0-312-28913-8	$11.95/$17.95 Can.

Variety Puzzles

Acrostic Puzzles Vol. 9	0-312-30949-X	$9.95/$14.95 Can.
Acrostic Puzzles Vol. 8	0-312-28410-1	$9.95/$14.95 Can.
Sunday Variety Puzzles	0-312-30059-X	$9.95/$14.95 Can.

Portable Size Format

Beach Bag Crosswords	0-312-31455-8	$6.95/$9.95 Can.
Crosswords for the Work Week	0-312-30952-X	$6.95/$9.95 Can.
Super Saturday	0-312-30604-0	$6.95/$9.95 Can.
Crosswords for the Holidays	0-312-30603-2	$6.95/$9.95 Can.
Sun, Sand, and Crosswords	0-312-30076-X	$6.95/$9.95 Can.
Weekend Challenge	0-312-30079-4	$6.95/$9.95 Can.
Crosswords for Your Coffee Break	0-312-28830-1	$6.95/$9.95 Can.

For Young Solvers

New York Times on the Web Crosswords for Teens	0-312-28911-1	$6.95/$9.95 Can.
Outrageous Crossword Puzzles and Word Games for Kids	0-312-28915-4	$6.95/$9.95 Can.
More Outrageous Crossword Puzzles for Kids	0-312-30062-X	$6.95/$9.95 Can.

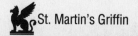
St. Martin's Griffin